CBT Toolbox
For
Children &
Adolescents

Over 200 Worksheets & Exercises
for Trauma, ADHD, Autism, Anxiety,
Depression & Conduct Disorders

LISA WEED PHIFER, DEd, NCSP
AMANDA K. CROWDER, MSW, LCSW
TRACY ELSENRAAT, MA, LPC, ATR-BC
ROBERT HULL, EDS, MEd, NCSP

Published by:
PESI Publishing & Media
PESI, Inc.
3839 White Ave.
Eau Claire, WI 54703

Cover Design: Amy Rubenzer
Editing By: Blair Davis
Layout: Amy Rubenzer & Mayfly Designs

Printed in the United States of America
ISBN: 9781683730750

PESI
Publishing
& Media
www.pesipublishing.com

Acknowledgments

In 2015, Hillary Jenness of PESI asked us to consider creating a book that would support therapists working with children who have emotional and behavioral disorders. We welcomed this opportunity and got right to work on creating this very practical book on activity-based cognitive behavioral therapy. We collaborated with colleagues of varying disciplines to create a workbook with engaging activities for clients, therapists, and caregivers. We want to express our sincere thanks and gratitude first to Hillary and PESI for this opportunity and also Sarah Porzig and Elissa Kauffman.

We would also like to acknowledge the many therapists and support people who dedicate their time, lives, and hearts to transforming the lives of children.

LISA WEED PHIFER, DEd, NCSP
AMANDA K. CROWDER, MSW, LCSW
TRACY ELSENRAAT, MA, LPC, ATR-BC
ROBERT HULL, EDS, Med, NCSP

Contents

Introduction xi

I. Childhood Trauma

Cognitive Skills

Thinking

Cognitive Behavioral Triangle 2
My Ouch Story 3
Safety Planning 4

Memory

Memory Cloud Walk 5
Memory Land 6
Creating a Schedule 7

Language

Communication Rules 8
This vs. That, Introduction 9
This vs. That 10
Say It Strong 14

Relationship Coaching

Alliance Building

Building a Bridge, Introduction 15
Building a Bridge, Part 1: Present 16
Building a Bridge, Part 2: Past 17
Building a Bridge, Part 3: Collaboration 18

Reciprocal Relationships

Moods and Relationships 19
Relationship Balance, Introduction 20
Relationship Balance 21
Relationship Roadblocks 22

Pro-social Skills

What Do You See? 23
Cycles of Relationships 24
Triggers and Shields, Introduction 25
Triggers and Shields 26

Competency Skills

Resilience

Power Poster, Introduction 27
Power Poster: Part 1 28
Power Poster: Part 2 29
My Positive Thought Journal 30

Symptom Relief

Boo Boos and Bandages 31
Coping Skills 32
Thermometer 33

Emotional Regulation

Feeling Faces 34
Feeling Pie 35
Comfort Levels 36

Brain-Based Learning

Connecting with the Present

Cleaning Up Negative Thoughts 37
Grounding Exercises 38
Balloon Breathing 39

Quieting the Body

Calm Images 40
Calm Down Plan 41
Roll a Brain Break! 42

Mind and Body

    Mind and Body Wellness Plan 43

    Connecting the Body with Emotions,

    Introduction 44

    Connecting the Body with Emotions 45

    Exercise Diary 46

II. Attention Deficit Hyperactivity Disorder

Cognitive Skills

Concentration

    Examining Inattention 48

    Distraction "To Do" List 49

    Times of Inattention 50

Impulse Control

    Examining Impulsivity 51

    Internal vs. External Distractions 52

    Back on Track! Coping with Distractions 53

    Creating a Schedule 54

Metacognition

    Finding a Solution 54

    Thinking About My Warning Signs 55

    Reframing Thoughts 56

Relationship Coaching

Alliance Building

    Family Rules 57

    End on a Good Note 58

    All or Nothing and Everything in Between 59

Reciprocal Relationships

    Say It or Swallow It 60

    Being a Good Friend 61

    Staying on Topic, Introduction 62

    Staying on Topic 63

Pro-social Skills

    Boundaries 64

    How Big Is My Problem? 65

    Does My Reaction Match My Problem? 66

Competency Skills

Time Management

    Estimating Time 67

    Goal Setting Worksheet 68

    Visualization of Distant Rewards 69

Self-Regulation

    Attention Regulator 70

    Action Regulator 71

    Stop and Think! Managing Impulsivity 72

Memory

    Breaking It Down 73

    Cues on Cards 74

    Cognitive Flexibility, Introduction 75

    Cognitive Flexibility 76

Brain-Based Learning

Brain Breaks

    Calm Down Bingo, Introduction 77

    Calm Down Bingo 78

    Animal Break Ladder 79

    Whole-Body Games 80

Healthy Habits

    Healthy Plate, Introduction 81

    Healthy Plate 82

    Exercise Routine 83

    Time for Bed 84

Positive Mindset

    Positive Self-Reflection Log 85

    Positive Imagery Practice: In Control

       and Focused 86

    Look at What I Accomplished! 87

III. Autism Spectrum Disorder

Cognitive Skills

Facilitating Conversation

    Allow Me to Introduce Myself,

    Introduction 90

    Allow Me to Introduce Myself 91

Conversation Map 92
    Conversation Toolkit 93

Flexible Thinking
    Flexible vs. Rigid Thinking 94
    Dealing with Detours 95
    Embracing Change 96

Sensory Integration
    Sensory Profile 97
    Sensory Awareness 98
    Sensory Escape 99

Relationship Coaching

Perspective
    Perceptive Taking 100
    Looking at All Sides 101
    Common Ground 102

Emotional Expression
    Emotions Cheat Sheet 103
    Understanding Emotions 104
    What's My Emotional Temperature? 105

Pro-social Skills
    Mindful Communication 106
    "I" Statement 101 107
    "I" Statements vs. "You" Statements 108

Competency Skills

Managing Expectations
    Is it an Emergency? 109
    Expected vs. Unexpected 110
    Examining Expectations 112

Functional Interactions
    My Personal Bubble 113
    Control My Volume 114
    Appropriate Touching 115

Thought Challenging
    Perseveration Log 116
    Perseveration Information 117
    Perseveration Action Plan, Introduction 118
    Perseveration Action Plan 119

Brain-Based Learning

Relaxation
    Cool Down Checklist 120
    Race Track Breathing: Warm Up or
    Cool Down 121
    Visual Breathing 122

Social Thinking
    How Can I Help? 123
    I CAN Make a Choice 125
    Reaching Out for Help 126

Brain Games
    Emotional Connection Game 127
    Find a Friend 128
    Conversation Cube 129

IV. Conduct Disorder

Cognitive Skills

Anger
    Getting to Know Your Anger 132
    Tackling Anger Mountain 133
    Weekly Anger Diary 134

Aggression
    Times of Acting Out: Introduction 135
    Times of Acting Out: Client 136
    Times of Acting Out: Caregiver 137
    Times of Acting Out: Plan of Action 138

Dysregulation
    Going Back in Time 139
    Recognizing Emotional Limits 140
    Body Reactions 141

Relationship Coaching

Communication
    I Feel 142
    Watch Your Words 143
    Communicating with Others 144

Alliance Building
    Understanding Family Rules 145
    Friends and Family 146

Respecting Myself and Others 147

Pro-social Skills

Pro-social Behaviors 148

Helpful Behaviors 149

Helpful Self 150

Competency Skills

Sequencing

Behavior Sequencing, Introduction 151

Behavior Sequencing: Part 1 152

Tipping Point: Part 2 153

Behavior Sequencing Redo: Part 3 154

Emotion Regulation

Control Cards 155

Reframing Thoughts 156

Change of Mind 157

Emotional Vocabulary

Building Emotional Vocabulary 158

Linking Emotions, Thoughts, and Feelings 159

Feeling States 160

Brain-Based Learning

Creating Peace

Peace Chain 161

Peaceful Actions 162

Thinking Peace 163

Body Control

Recipe for Success 164

Yell It from the Mountaintop 165

10-Point Check-In 166

Gratitude

Letter of Thanks 167

Little Victories 168

Grateful Feelings 169

V. Anxiety

Cognitive Skills

Defining Anxiety

Getting to Know Your Worry 172

Anxiety Hierarchy, Introduction 173

Anxiety Hierarchy 174

Your Worry 175

Thought Distortion

"Good" Worry vs. "Bad" Worry 176

Detective 177

Weighing Your Worries 178

Physical Reactions/Somatization

Responses, Reactions, and Feelings 179

How Do You Respond to Your Worry? 180

Thoughts and Feelings Log 181

Relationship Coaching

Alliance Building

Talking with Others 182

Helpful Thinking 183

Trust Bubble 184

Assertiveness

Assertiveness Regulator 185

Three Wishes 186

To Do, Won't Do List 187

Pro-social Skills

Pro-social Behaviors 188

Stressed Out! 189

Fear/Anxiety Self-Statements 190

Competency Skills

Problem Solving

Red Light, Yellow Light, Green Light 191

Creating Your Own Coping Kit 192

Stay Calm Checklist 193

Control

Circle of Control 194

Managing Expectations of Control 195

Controlling Your Thoughts 196

Thought Challenging

What Will Work? 197

How Do We Get There? 198

Stop, Rewind, Rethink, Introduction 199

Stop, Rewind, Rethink 200

Brain-Based Learning

Positive Changes

    Within Reach! 201

    26 Positive Traits 202

    Self-Care Routine 203

Perspective Changing

    Staying in the Present, Introduction 204

    Staying in the Present 205

    Let's Box It Away 206

    You're Not Alone 207

Brain Games

    Relaxation Rolls 208

    Mandala 209

    Anxiety the Alien, Introduction 210

    Anxiety the Alien 211

VI. Depression

Cognitive Skills

Mood

    Understanding Your Mood 214

    Mood Tracking 215

    Building Your Defense, Introduction 216

    Building Your Defense 217

Isolation

    Social Interaction and Mood 218

    People Around Me 219

    Support Chain 220

Emotional Expression

    My Feelings 221

    Uncut Diamond 222

    Inside Out 223

Relationship Coaching

Confidence

    I Am 224

    Your Inner You 225

    Self-Portrait 226

Supportive Alliance

    Supportive Responses 227

    Understanding Stress and Support 228

    Support Constellation 229

Self-Esteem

    I Like Me! 230

    Awards, Introduction 231

    Awards 232

    I Am Valuable 233

Competency Skills

Realistic Thinking

    Reframing Sad Thoughts 234

    Optimistic Views 235

    Test Your Thinking 236

Coping

    Positive Self-Talk, Introduction 237

    Positive Self-Talk 238

    The Four Questions 239

    Coping Skills Tree 240

Problem Solving

    Stoplight Problem Solving 241

    Finding Another Solution 242

    Reaching Out 243

Brain-Based Learning

Fostering Motivation

    What Drives You? 244

    Positive Goal Setting 245

    Self-Improvement Plan 246

Positive Changes

    Connecting with Your Body 247

    Making Positive Changes 248

    Self-Care Plan 249

Healthy Body

    Get Moving! 250

    Sleep Schedule 251

    Emotional Eating 252

Introduction

CBT Toolbox for Children and Adolescents was designed with therapists in mind to provide brief, targeted solutions to a myriad of mental health issues that are frequently present in children. The activities in this workbook enhance traditional CBT by promoting the development of a child's executive functioning, developing social skills, and prompting whole brain approach. Traditional therapy relies heavily on language and the activities in this book accompany language with nonverbal activities to help facilitate growth with individuals who have difficulties reflecting and changing their own negative thinking. This book used a multidisciplinary approach relying on the expertise of school psychologists, social workers and therapists. We have put together an abundance of creative ideas that can engage and inspire allowing clients to express themselves, communicate with others and create positive change.

The workbook covers six clinical areas: Childhood Trauma, Attention Deficit Hyperactivity Disorder, Autism Spectrum Disorder, Conduct Disorder, Anxiety, and Depression. The activities are tailored to specific disorders and symptomology and can be combined to meet the client's needs in regards to interrupting negative thought patterns, developing healthy relationships, and creating a mind-body connection. Within each chapter are four content areas tailored to the specific disorder.

1. **Cognitive Skills**
   These activities focus on recognizing symptoms, determining the impact of negative thinking patterns, and enhancing memory strategies.

2. **Relationship Coaching**
   These activities focus on the development of pro-social behavior, building alliances, and improving interpersonal relationships.

3. **Competency Building**
   These activities target emotional regulation, realistic thinking, coping, and problem solving.

4. **Brain-Based Learning**
   These activities focus on developing a mind-body connection, finding motivation, and developing healthy mental and physical habits.

How to Use this Book

This workbook provides activities to address countless symptoms with skill-building exercises. You will notice three types of worksheets: In-session Exercise, Client Activity and Caregiver Worksheet. These handouts have different uses and each one is written from a different perspective.

In-session Exercises are designed for the therapist to use as a tool while in-session. Including the client, caregiver and therapist in one setting, they are made to spark conversation and make the client comfortable.

Client Activities are created for the child to do themselves either in-session or as homework. Whether supervised by the therapist or their caregiver, they will be able to do the activity at any age or stage in the treatment process.

Caregiver Worksheets are for the parent or caregiver-to help them cope and work with the therapist, and also allow them to become part of the therapy process and reinforce strategies being taught in-session.

Although suggestions, ideas, and specific instructions are given, we encourage creativity within your own setting and specialty. These activities can be used to engage children directly in therapy, used in a group format for at-risk children, or as a strength building competency activity. As every therapist knows, skills that are repetitively practiced outside of therapy have a greater chance of being retained and used when faced with challenges.

Think Outside the PAGE

Let these activities act as a springboard to your own creativity. All these activities can be adapted to meet your client's age, developmental capacity, or current stage in treatment. It is important to let the client dictate when a piece is completed and how much they would like to expand the given directive. If a client is invested in a certain activity, you may consider letting him or her work on it over several sessions to maximize your information gathering. A loosely structured approach allows more opportunities for your client to encounter challenges in the process, which will result in opportunities for problem solving, skill building, and relationship building. Keep in mind that once an activity is completed, the client's processing of those skills continues.

Go Beyond the Activity Itself!

The activity or art piece is significantly important to the therapeutic process, the dialogue about the activity is equally important. Consider having the client title each activity and journal about it. Engage in discussions with the client regarding his or her feelings about this process of creating by using nonjudgmental commentary and open-ended questioning.

The artwork is an extension of self to be honored; therefore, it is important to have a plan for what to do with completed pieces to honor them and protect them. This ritual offers closure to the creative process. Options to consider include creating a portfolio to keep in the office until treatment is ended or for the client to take home. You may also find a safe place for the artwork to be on display in the office or use the artwork in other treatment activities; for example, many of the pieces created in session would double nicely as a focal point for guided imagery activities. The artwork could also be used in the client's home as a daily reminder of skills to practice or as a banner of pride and accomplishment. Process these options with the client ahead of time and come to an agreed plan.

Keep in mind that once an activity is completed, the client's processing of those skills continues. There are therapeutic advantages to repeating activities at different points in the therapeutic process. You might consider having the client do the activity again in the same way it was done before and then process the differences. Another option would be to complete a similar version of the activity to better meet where the client is at that particular point in treatment. Both options offer the client opportunity for repetition and mastery.

Childhood Trauma

This chapter will assist with developing a person's ability to be resilient and overcome adverse experiences, introducing the concept that the job of the caregiver, child and therapist is to impact the subjective meaning of events that enables a child to move from being overwhelmed by an event to having an event empower them into resilience and growth. These exercises focus on dealing with feelings of guilt, blame and loss, the ability to use emotional energy in a positive way, and improve relationships so they can feel accepted. (Every child's response to these activities will differ; sometimes a person's response differs from what you think it should be.)

Cognitive Behavioral Triangle

This activity will bring awareness of how our thoughts, feelings, and behaviors are connected, and identify how negative events can change our thinking patterns. Identify two positive events and two negative events and complete the spaces below. Discuss this with your therapist; your thoughts about it, your feelings related to it, and how these both may affect your behaviors.

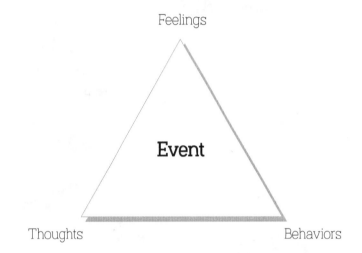

Event	Thoughts	Feelings	Behaviors
Negative			
Negative			
Positive			
Positive			

My Ouch Story

Everyone has a story to tell. When bad things happen, it makes it much harder to tell the story. When bad things happen to us, there is typically a lot of shame, guilt, and embarrassment. This activity provides guidance to achieve the goal of telling your story without the shame, guilt, and embarrassment. To get the story out, so that someone else can hear it and read it. Complete the sentences below with your story. Please use additional pages as needed.

I remember a time when _____

_____

First, _____

_____

Next I remember _____

_____

Then, _____

_____

Last, _____

_____

I remember feeling _____

I would like to feel _____

I need _____ because _____

_____

I feel safe when _____

These are the people in my life who support me _____

_____

When I get upset, I can _____

_____ to feel safe again.

Safety Planning

1. What are your trauma reminders or triggers? (Please circle all that apply)

    Being touched   Being isolated   Specific person (Who)
    Time of year (When)   People in uniform   Anniversaries (What)
    Particular time of day Yelling/fighting   People being too close
    (When)   Being forced to talk   Other: _____
    Not having input   Being around men/women
    Bedroom door open or closed   Seeing others out of control

2. Please describe your warning signs; for example, what your body feels when you are losing control, and what other people can see changing? (Please circle all that apply)

    Sweating   Isolating self   Being agitated
    Red faced   Eating less   Clenching fists
    Rocking   Racing heart   Bouncing legs Swearing
    Crying   Loud voice   Nauseous
    Sleeping less   Eating more   Short of breath
    Breathing hard   Clenching teeth   Other: _____
    Wringing hands   Sleeping a lot
    Pacing   Can't sit still

3. What helps you feel or stay safe? (Please circle all that apply)

    Writing   Walking   Exercise/sports
    TV/movie   Reading   Drawing/coloring
    Listening to music   Video games   Taking a shower
    Support from peers   Talking with adults   Other: _____

4. What helps you stay in control? _____

   _____

5. What helped you stay in control in the past? _____

   _____

6. What kind of space is most comfortable when you need it? _____

   _____

Memory Cloud Walk

Write down past challenges and how you solved them. Questions to think about: What happened? What did you do? Did anyone help you? Are there any similarities? What did you learn? Has anything changed over time? What does this say about you?

Memory #1:

Solution:

Support:

Memory #2:

Solution:

Support:

Memory #3:

Solution:

Support:

Memory #4:

Solution:

Support:

Memory Land

Memories can be hard but are useful in helping us understand and battle our fears. Sometimes we may tend to ignore things that are painful and other times it may be hard to stop thinking about them. Use the organizer below to recall details of memories so you can identify your feelings and move toward healing.

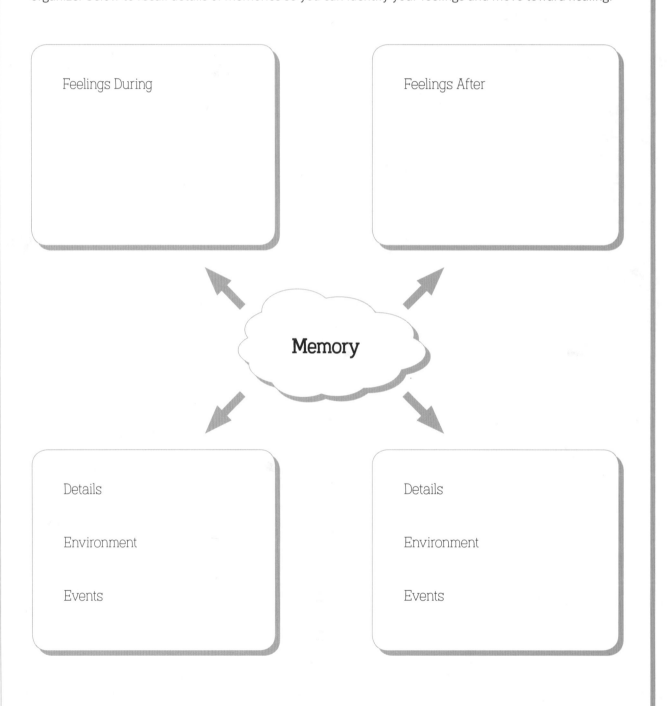

Feelings During

Feelings After

Memory

Details

Environment

Events

Details

Environment

Events

Creating a Schedule

Consistency and structure are very important for children and adolescents, especially when a trauma has occurred. Typically, when a trauma occurs, the person is left feeling out of control. Creating a schedule is a helpful way to increase structure and predictability. Work with your child to create a schedule for daily activities and discuss alternatives to handling changes in routine.

	Monday	Tuesday	Wednesday	Thursday	Friday	Saturday	Sunday
6 AM– 8 AM							
8 AM– 10 AM							
10 AM– 12 PM							
12 PM– 2 PM							
2 PM– 4 PM							
4 PM– 6 PM							
6 PM– 8 PM							
8 PM– 10 PM							

Communication Rules

Make copies of the scroll below for both caregiver and child to complete.

Make a list of rules for the other person to keep in mind when communicating or settling disputes. Think of behaviors or phrases that the other person can utilize to help you feel respected and validated. Be specific. Share your list once completed.

Therapist Note: When discussing the list, point out similarities and differences among the rules. How realistic are the requests? If something is not realistic, help client revise to make it more appropriate.

This vs. That

Communication between family members, especially parent and child, can be difficult particularly when dealing with trauma. This vs. That is a guided activity designed to help facilitate communication between the caregiver and child. The caregiver and the child will have an opportunity to reflect on each other's strengths as well as problematic behaviors. The caregiver and child questionnaire on pages 10-13 can be completed by the individual or can be completed as an interview. When both are finished filling out the forms, discuss the similarities and differences in both surveys. Recognize the strengths of both and acknowledge behaviors that need to be changed.

This vs. That

Caregiver Perspective

1. What are some positives you can identify about your child?

_____

_____

_____

2. Why are these positives or things that you like to see?

_____

_____

_____

3. What are the negative behaviors you can identify?

_____

_____

_____

4. Why are these negatives or things that you do not like to see?

_____

_____

_____

5. What is the biggest change that you would like to see as it relates to your child?

_____

_____

_____

6. What are some things that you think you can improve on as a caregiver?

_____

_____

_____

7. What are some things that you think you do well as a caregiver?

_____

_____

_____

_____

This vs. That

Client Perspective

1. What are some positives that you can identify about your parent/caregiver?

_____

_____

_____

_____

2. Why do you like these things?

_____

_____

_____

_____

3. What are some things that you do not like your parent/caregiver doing?

_____

_____

_____

_____

4. Why don't you like these things?

_____

_____

_____

_____

5. What is the biggest change that you would like to see?

_____

_____

_____

6. What behaviors would you identify as negative within yourself?

_____

_____

_____

_____

7. Why do you think these are negative behaviors?

_____

_____

_____

8. What do you think you do well?

_____

_____

_____

Say It Strong

Mirror, mirror on the wall. Saying positive things will help you feel tall. Write statements of praise and encouragement in the mirror below. Recite these phrases daily to help set a positive mindset.

Building a Bridge

Building a Bridge is a three-part activity. Review with the client the instructions listed on each of the following three pages one at a time. Do not move on to the next step until the previous step has been completed. The client should be in agreement as to when an activity or image has reached completion.

After each part is completed, challenge your client to engage in discussion and describe his/her image. Ask the client about the feelings they experience when they view the completed image. You might also invite the client to give each part a title and offer time to journal about the activity and the image created before moving on to the next step. To assist in this process, you will find dialogue questions at the bottom of the page for each of these three parts.

Once completing Part 3, you could expand the exercise by offering for the client and caregiver to collaborate in filling the space under the bridge with "obstacles" from life that seem to create challenges for the client to move through to the other side of healing.

Building a Bridge

Part 1: Present

Draw an image of a landscape in the box below that depicts how your current life feels. Keep in mind current challenges or feelings.

```
┌─────────────────────────────────────────────┐
│          Part 1: How I Feel Right Now         │
│                                               │
│                                               │
│                                               │
│                                               │
│                                               │
│                                               │
│                                               │
│                                               │
│                                               │
│                                               │
│                                               │
│                                               │
│                                               │
│                                               │
│                                               │
└─────────────────────────────────────────────┘
```

Describe your image. What feelings do you have when you look at this image?

_____

_____

_____

Building a Bridge

Part 2: Future

Draw a landscape image in the box below that depicts how you would like your life to look and feel after you have healed from this trauma.

Part 2: How I Will Feel After Healing

Describe your image. How will you feel, and who or what will help you cope with future challenges?

_____

_____

_____

Building a Bridge

Part 3: Collaboration

Enlist the help of a caregiver or another supportive individual. Work together on building a bridge to connect your two images from Parts 1 and 2. Consider using additional art supplies such as twigs, paper towel tubes, popsicle sticks, pipe cleaners, twisted or crumbled sheets of paper, or other found materials. Be as creative as you would like.

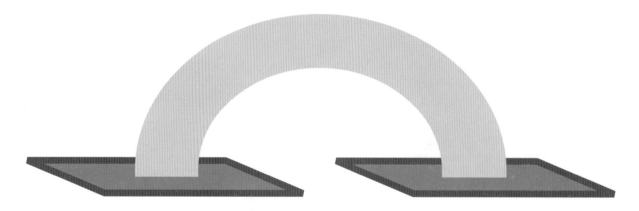

Describe your decision-making skills in designing and building this bridge. What was it like to work together on this project? How did you offer each other support? Do you think this bridge is sturdy? Discuss or draw possible obstacles toward healing under the bridge. Discuss the ways your caregiver and other supports in your life will help support the "bridge" during the healing process.

_____

_____

_____

_____

_____

_____

_____

_____

Moods and Relationships

Think of a relationship that is important to you or one that you would like to work on making better. Explore how your mood and behaviors are preventing you from being the person you would like to be in this relationship. Describe how you would like to contribute to this relationship.

The Relationship

How Your Mood and Behaviors Get in the Way

Why is this relationship significant to you?

How has your mood prevented you from contributing to this relationship the way you would like?

How does the other person respond to your mood and behaviors?

Describe the contributions you would like to make to this relationship.

The Way You Would Like it to Be

Relationship Balance

To begin this exercise, you will need to make two copies of the following page. One copy will be for the caregiver to complete and the other will be for the client. Review the instructions on the page with the client and caregiver. Once the exercise is completed, invite each person to share his or her completed exercise. Then, begin a dialogue to explore each person's observations. After your group discussion, consider offering the client and caregiver an opportunity to journal about their observations and their thoughts about moving forward.

Follow-Up Questions

- What observations were made about each list?
- What similarities and differences can be found?
- What efforts would help each side of the relationship feel balanced?
- How realistic are those expectations?
- What efforts could be made today to reach a better balance?

Relationship Balance

In the shaded box below, list what the OTHER person offers to this relationship. For example, if you are the caregiver, you would list in this box what your child offers to your relationship.

In the white box, list what YOU offer to this relationship.

Think about whether or not you feel this relationship is balanced. If not, use the triangle below to list what efforts could be made to help achieve a better balance in this relationship.

Once your exercise is completed, share and discuss your observations.

Relationship Roadblocks

Think of your relationships as a journey. What roadblocks are standing in the way of building healthy relationships? Depict these as bumps, detours, or other obstructions. Draw or write their names in the symbols below. Think about how these issues can be resolved or prevented. What actions can you take right now?

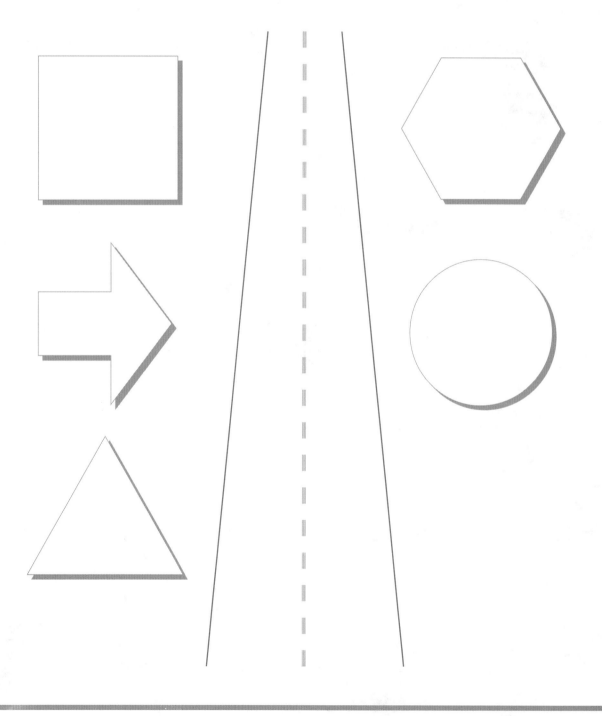

What Do You See?

When bad things happen to us, we tend to blame ourselves. This activity helps deconstruct negative self-views and promote positive thoughts. Fold the paper in half on the dotted line. Draw a picture of how others see you. Then draw a picture of how you see yourself. Open the paper and compare the two drawings.

How Others See You

What qualities and traits would others say you possess? How do you feel about this image of yourself? How accurate is their view of you? What would you like to change about their perception of you?

How You See Yourself

What qualities and traits do you possess? How do you feel about this image of yourself?
What would you like to change about your perception of yourself?
What differences do you notice between these two drawings and their titles?

Cycles of Relationships

Therapist note: Give a copy of this worksheet to both the child and caregiver to complete separately.

Think of a hurdle in your relationship together. In the arrow on the left, list your behaviors. In the arrow on the right, list the other person's responses/behaviors. Notice how one response or behavior might lead to the other and cause a repeating pattern. In the space in the middle, list how this cycle could be stopped from repeating. When finished, share and compare each cycle drawing.

What similarities and differences can be found? What efforts would help each of you to feel heard and validated? What efforts could you each make today to best support each other?

Triggers and Shields

To begin this exercise, review the instructions on the following page with the client. Consider making as many copies of this page as needed to address each trigger individually.

The client might experience challenges in identifying "triggers." If you encounter this issue, engage the client in dialogue about what events or experiences seem to occur just before a particular trigger feeling/behavior.

If the client experiences challenges in developing a "shield," engage him/her in discussion to explore how to prevent escalation and negative self-talk.

After the client has completed the exercise, engage in continued discussion about the identified triggers and shields that were created. Consider offering the client an opportunity to journal about this experience and his/her observations. Use the following questions to assist your dialogue and journaling:

- What positive outcomes can occur when you use your shield – to include thoughts, feelings, and interactions with others?

- What would your shield be made out of?

- What protective qualities would it possess?

- Where would you like to carry or use this shield?

- What would it feel like after you use your shield for protection?

Triggers and Shields

In the box on the left, draw or write triggers experienced at home or school. Next, imagine if you could use a shield to protect yourself from these feelings and draw or write your shields in the box on the right.

TRIGGERS

SHIELD

Power Poster Part 1

The following exercise is a two part exercise. It will be a collaborative effort between the client and caregiver. In Power Poster Part 1, instruct the pair to work together in making a poster to depict and label the child's positive attributes. You might consider using larger paper if needed. Once the activity is completed, invite the client and caregiver to present their poster. Begin dialogue about what they chose to depict. Ask them to identify and explain the strengths and attributes that were depicted.

Follow Up: What strengths and positive attributes have been identified?
How could the child use these strengths when experiencing anxiety or difficulties?

Power Poster Part 2

In Power Poster Part 2, instruct the client and caregiver to list the positive attributes from the poster onto this new worksheet. Then, list a positive behavior that is associated with each attribute. This worksheet will then be used as a behavior chart to measure how often the child engages in the positive behaviors listed. Make as many of these sheets as needed to measure progress for each day.

Discuss examples of the child's behaviors that relate to their positive attributes.

• When could the child engage in these positive behaviors?

• Could these positive behaviors be used to help others?

• Could they be used to help the child when they are feeling low?

Complete periodic check-ins (and enlist the help of caregiver) to measure the child's progress in regularly engaging in these behaviors.

Power Poster

(Part 1)

—

Work together with your caregiver to create a Power Poster to depict and label positive attributes that you possess. Give your poster a title.

Power Poster
(Part 2)

Power Poster Positive Attribute (e.g., Thoughtful)	Behavior (e.g., Do a kind deed for a friend or family member.)	☺

My Positive Thought Journal

When you have a negative thought, write it down. Then change it to a positive thought.

Positive thought examples:

- I am good at …
- I have family who support me …
- I like …

Day	Negative Thought	Positive Thought
Sunday	*Example:* Something bad will happen.	*Example:* I am looking forward to …

Boo Boos and Bandages

Draw your sad feelings or thoughts on a separate piece of paper. These feelings will represent your boo boos. Write or draw healing messages on the bandages below. Cut out the bandages and paste or tape them over the boo boos.

Coping Skills

When you experience or are exposed to traumatic events often need to be reminded of those who support them, how to calm down, and where they feel safe. Coping cue cards can be tailored to meet the individual needs of the child. These small cards can be kept in your pocket or journal and easily accessed.

Who Loves Me?	Safety Looks and Feels Like:
This Makes Me Feel Calm:	I Enjoy:

Thermometer

The thermometer is a helpful symbol for you to express which situations cause the most tension. Give an example for each of the following numbers on the thermometer and select a color to represent how it feels.

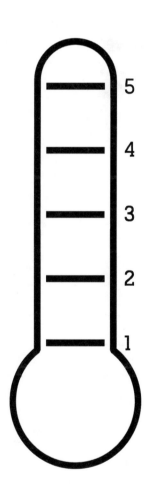

5 I feel overwhelmed. I want to get out of here!

_____

_____

4 I feel very uncomfortable. I need help.

_____

_____

3 I feel challenged but I can make it.

_____

_____

2 I feel comfortable. I can do this.

_____

_____

1 I feel very relaxed. No worries.

_____

_____

Feeling Faces

Look in a mirror. What feeling faces can you make? Draw some of those feeling faces below (e.g., happy, mad, sad, angry, surprised) and label them. After you've drawn your feeling faces, answer the following questions. When do you feel this way? How do you act and what do you say when you feel this?

> *Examples:* Happy, Sad, Surprised, Afraid, Worried, Tired, Melancholy, Mad, Calm, Content, Frustrated, Indifferent, Scared, Upset, Excited

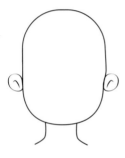

_____

_____

_____

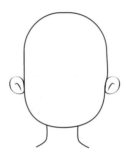

_____

_____

_____

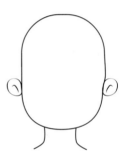

_____

_____

_____

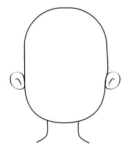

_____

_____

_____

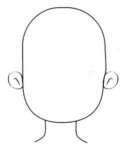

_____

_____

_____

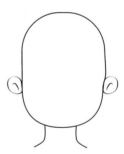

_____

_____

_____

Feeling Pie

A pie chart can help you visualize how you feel in different situations. The circle represents you. Color a slice of pie to represent how much of each feeling you are experiencing before your session and then after your session. What emotions do you feel before your sessions? Which emotion is the largest piece of the pie (e.g., happy, worried, sad, angry, etc.)? What emotion do you feel the most at the end of a session? Make that emotion your larger piece of the pie.

Before the Session

After the Session

Comfort Levels

Think of a comforting/soothing feeling. Write that feeling in the box to the left of the figure below. Then decide where in your body you experience that feeling. Use colors, shapes, and/or imagery inside the figure to show how that feeling feels inside your body.

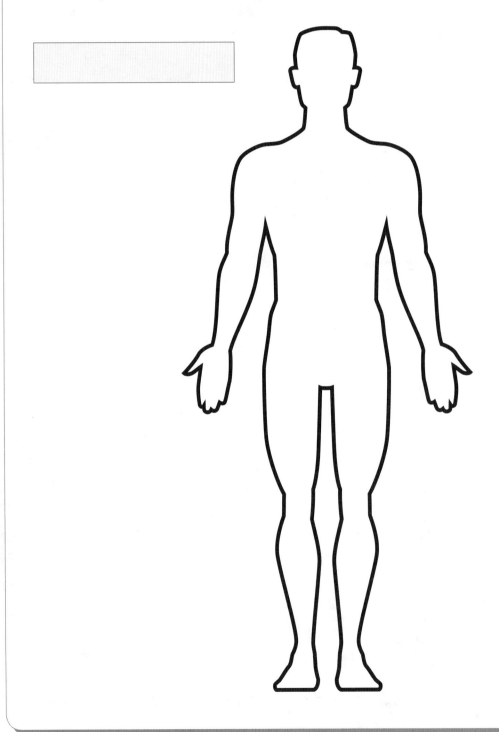

Cleaning Up Negative Thoughts

1. Write down a negative or long-lasting thought that is bothering you.
2. Crumple up the paper.
3. Say something positive to yourself.
4. Imagine throwing the negative thought into the trash can picture to relieve yourself of it.

TRASH CAN

Grounding Exercises

Individuals who experience traumatic events or traumatic stress may experience triggers when they are outside of therapy or away from home. It is important for children to practice grounding techniques to help them calm themselves, refocus attention to the present, and regain a feeling of safety.

Following are a few examples of quick grounding exercises to practice in the session. These can be written on a card and kept in the client's pocket.

Example 1:
5, 4, 3, 2, 1
Think of five things you can see, four things you can touch, three things you can hear, two things you can smell, one thing you can taste.

Example 2:
Positive Coping Mantra
"I am safe. I am [name], I am safe right now; this is just a memory. That was then, and this is now. I am in [place], and the date is [date]. This flashback will pass."

Balloon Breathing

When we are faced with upsetting thoughts or memories, controlled breathing can help calm our bodies and let us become mindful of our actions. To practice deep breathing, have the child breathe in. When they breathe out, have them pretend that they are blowing up a balloon. To help them control their breath, have them color the following balloons as they breathe out.

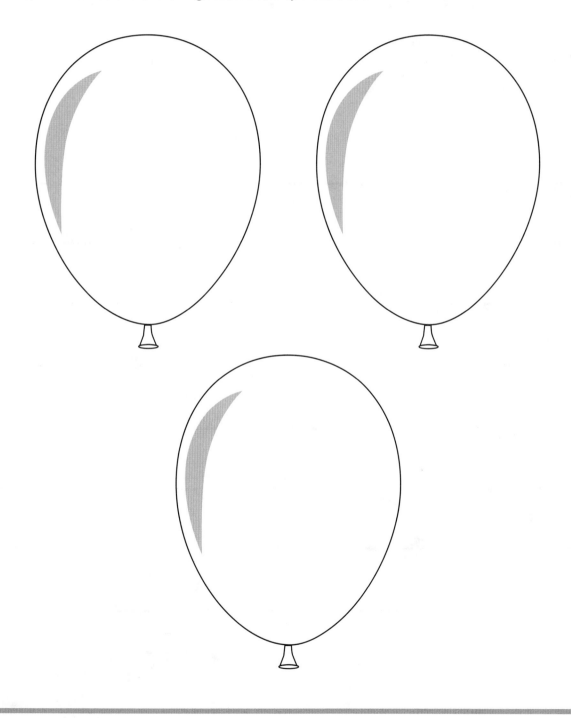

Calm Images

Materials: Paper, paint/crayons/markers, paintbrush.

Have the child think about colors and how each one can elicit a reaction. (Keep in mind that not everyone has the same reaction to specific colors.) Have the child choose colors that feel calming/soothing to them and create a picture on a separate piece of paper with those colors to represent the feeling of relaxation.

When the child completes the activity:

- Ask them to describe their image and why it feels relaxing.
- Discuss what activities they do in day-to-day life to elicit relaxation.
- Talk about how they can incorporate more opportunities to relax during their day.

_____

_____

_____

_____

_____

_____

_____

Calm Down Plan

This activity will help the child develop a quick visual reminder of how to settle down when faced with triggers. Have the child brainstorm preferred strategies and create a small illustration or use a color to help calm themselves. Following is an example of a four-step process.

Example:

Calm Down Plan
1. Sit down
2. Close eyes
3. Take 5 deep breaths
4. Get back to work

Create Your Own:

Calm Down Plan
1.
2.
3.
4.

Roll a Brain Break!

Encourage "brain breaks" during your session. Cut out the outline and fold and tape it to create a break cube. Have the client roll the cube and perform the task that they roll to help them refocus and connect with therapy.

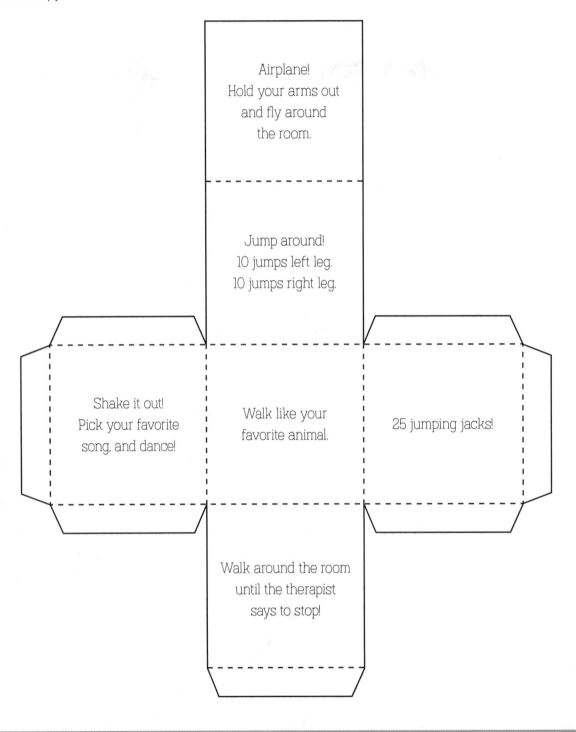

Airplane!
Hold your arms out
and fly around
the room.

Jump around!
10 jumps left leg.
10 jumps right leg.

Shake it out!
Pick your favorite
song, and dance!

Walk like your
favorite animal.

25 jumping jacks!

Walk around the room
until the therapist
says to stop!

Mind and Body Wellness Plan

Date: _____

MIND:
What are you going
to do this week to create a
healthy mind?

_____
_____
_____
_____
_____
_____

BODY:
What are you going
to do this week to create a
healthy body?

_____
_____
_____
_____
_____
_____

Personal goal for this week: _____

Triggers to avoid: _____

Coping skills to use: _____

End-of-the-week review. Please rate each of the following from 1 (not successful) to 5 (very successful):

Working toward my personal goal	1	2	3	4	5
Avoiding triggers	1	2	3	4	5
Using coping skills	1	2	3	4	5
Bettering my mind and body	1	2	3	4	5

Connecting the Body with Emotions

Connecting the Body with Emotions worksheet is designed to help the client connect their physical actions and reactions with emotions. Have the client describe a memory or situation that was upsetting. Then have the client color in the body next to it using a color that indicates how and what their body feels when it's in "fight or flight" mode.

Next, ask the client to describe a physical activity(s) that would help them release the tension from the upsetting memories. (For example: I feel anger in my face and want to yell, so I could scream into my pillow.) Have them color the second body picture to indicate how their body feels when engaged in the positive physical activity.

Connecting the Body with Emotions

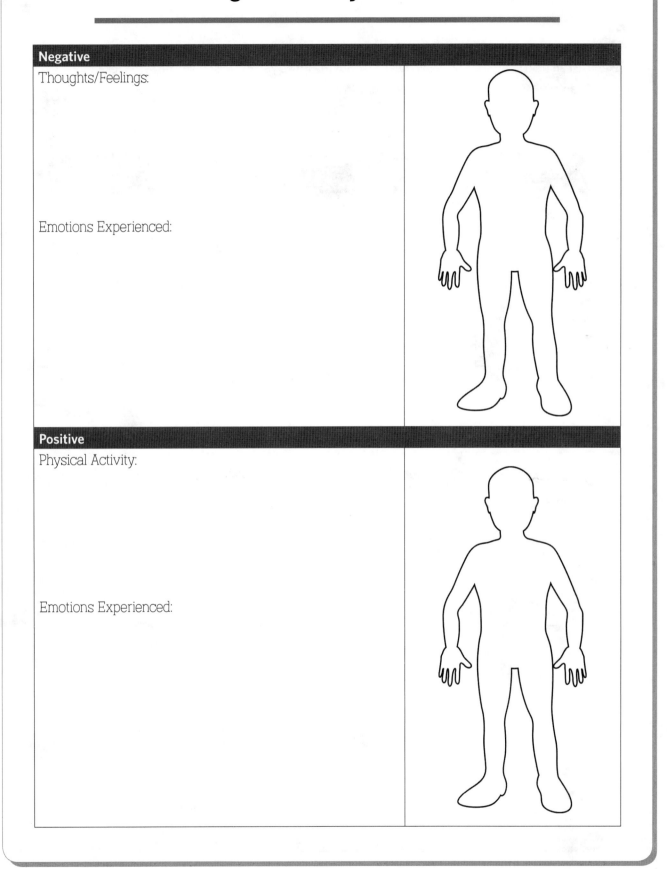

Negative

Thoughts/Feelings:

Emotions Experienced:

Positive

Physical Activity:

Emotions Experienced:

■ 45

Exercise Diary

Exercise can help improve well-being. Keep track of the times you exercised and how you felt before and after. Example: Were you having a stressful day? Were you able to think more clearly after walking for 30 minutes?

Date	How Did You Feel Before?	Type of Exercise & Duration	How Did You Feel After?

Attention Deficit Hyperactivity Disorder

ctivities in this chapter help to define symptoms and understand the impact on daily living. The activities are organized by the skills needed to mitigate and control the impact of symptomatology on social and academic performance. Developing a better understanding of symptoms will help facilitate client awareness of how thoughts and actions are connected. Relationships coaching activities focus on developing appropriate social boundaries, understanding expectations and engaging in socially-appropriate behaviors. Competency-based activities concentrate on adaptive and executive functioning such as estimating time, self-regulation, and understanding the impact of their actions. Brain-based interventions conclude the chapter providing activities that integrate healthy habits, using positive imagery, and using physical movement to help reduce symptoms.

Examining Inattention

What Does Inattention Look Like?

What does being inattentive mean to you? Describe what inattention looks like in each of the following settings. Are there places where you are more focused? Are there places where you are more inattentive?

HOME	SCHOOL	COMMUNITY

How Does Inattention Impact Me?

How does being inattentive impact you in each of these settings? When does being inattentive impact your performance the most? What are the negative and positive consequences of being impulsive?

HOME	SCHOOL	COMMUNITY

Distraction "To Do" List

While working do you have difficulty blocking out invading thoughts? When the off-task thoughts occur, do you become distracted and have a hard time getting back to the task at hand? When you have an invading thought write it down, and then address it after your work is complete.

1. _____

2. _____

3. _____

4. _____

5. _____

6. _____

7. _____

8. _____

Review the list with your caregiver. Which of these thoughts are important and need to be addressed immediately? Which thoughts can be ignored or put off for now?

Times of Inattention

Write down a schedule of a typical day for your child. You can make extra copies of this schedule to reflect weekend versus school days. Identify which times of day your child has the most trouble with attention and focus and make a note next to the activities they do at those times.

Time of Day	Activity	Consequences

Examining Impulsivity

What Does Impulsivity Look Like?

What does impulsivity mean to you? Describe what impulsive behaviors might look like in each of the following settings. When are you more in control? When do you feel less in control?

HOME	SCHOOL	COMMUNITY

How Does Impulsivity Impact Me?

How does acting impulsively impact me in each of these settings? When does impulsivity impact performance the most? What are the negative and positive consequences of being impulsive?

HOME	SCHOOL	COMMUNITY

Internal vs. External Distractions

Throughout the day, we are presented with tons of distractions (e.g., noises, thoughts, others talking). It is important to recognize what types of distractions are experienced throughout the day. List the distractions that occur inside your body and outside your body.

Internal Distractions (Inside Me)	External Distractions (Outside Me)

Back on Track! Coping with Distractions

Look back at your *Internal vs. External Distractions* worksheet. What coping skills can you use when the distractions occur?

Internal Distractor	Coping Skills

External Distractor	Coping Skills

Finding a Solution

There are often several ways to solve a problem. Identify a current problem and brainstorm two solutions. What are the potential positive and negative outcomes of each solution? Below the chart, indicate the best solution to your problem and why it works.

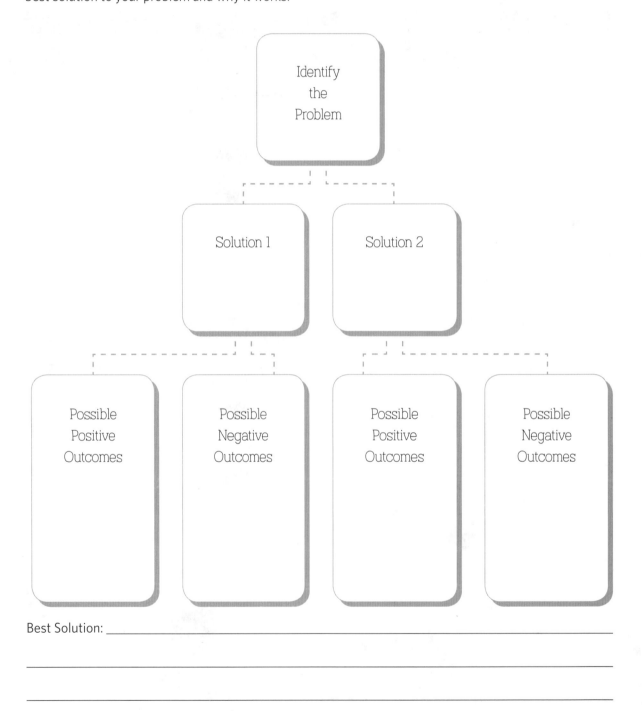

Best Solution: _____

_____

_____

Thinking About My Warning Signs

How do you feel about and what do you think about your individual warning signs? What do others feel and think about them?

My Warning Signs (e.g., fidgety, off task, talkative, daydreaming, overwhelmed, quiet, stressed)	What I Think/ Feel About Them	What Others Think/ Feel About Them

Reframing Thoughts

Cognitive distortions (e.g., "I'm not good enough," "I'm a failure") can impact our daily functioning. Work with the client and/or caregiver to identify a negative thought. Discuss how changing the thought will positively impact future thinking, feeling, and behavior?

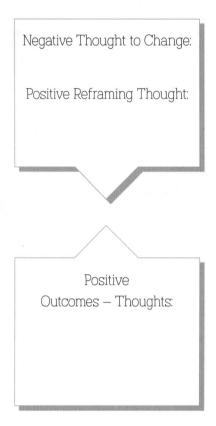

Negative Thought to Change:

Positive Reframing Thought:

Positive
Outcomes – Thoughts:

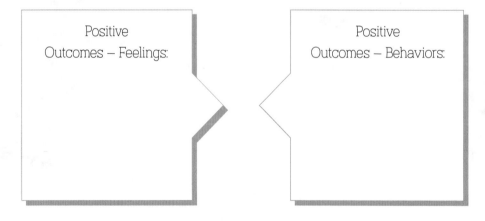

Positive
Outcomes – Feelings:

Positive
Outcomes – Behaviors:

Family Rules

You and the child should identify one to three rules that need to be followed at home. Make sure the rules are worded so that the child fully understands expectations. With each rule identify the daily or weekly reward for complying (e.g., stickers, snack, activity time, game night, etc.). Also, discuss the consequences for not following the rule (e.g., time out, reduced activity time, additional chores, etc.).

Family Rule	Reward	Consequence
1.		
2.		
3.		

End on a Good Note

Throughout the day, look for positive behaviors from the child and make note of them here. You may point out these positive behaviors and offer praise as they are noticed throughout the day. At the end of the day, you and the child will review the list. Repeat this activity for as many days as necessary.

What are the identified positive behaviors? Do you need assistance looking for and identifying positive behaviors? Ask for the child's feedback regarding feelings on being praised for specific behaviors and how it feels to review all of the praises from the day.

All or Nothing
and Everything in Between

Below, write down the client's strengths and weaknesses. Then define a recent problem they have experienced (e.g., studying for tests, making friends, calling out in class). How can they use a specific strength to help improve a weakness? Complete the task below.

Example:

Problem: John has difficulty studying for tests. When he studies, he reads the information but can not remember it well. He says that he is just bad at taking tests.

Strength:	Creating songs
Weakness:	Remembering facts for an exam
Using Strength to Compensate:	Make a song to remember material for test

Problem:

Strength:

Weakness:

Using Strength to Compensate:

Say It or Swallow It

Just because we think it, that doesn't mean we should say it. Review the following questions and decide if you should say it or swallow it!

	Say It	Swallow It
I like how you did your hair today.		
Why are you wearing those glasses?		
Why are your teeth crooked?		
I like your other shoes better.		
Want to play a game with me?		
Can you help me with my work?		
I like the color of your shirt.		
Add your own:		

Being a Good Friend

Actions speak louder than words. What do our actions say to our friends? Review the list that follows and decide whether or not each action goes with being a good friend.

Using praise	Grabbing	Interrupting	Yelling
Invading space	Giving a thumps up	Using a loud voice	Listening
Making noises	Saying "Excuse me"	Waiting your turn	Smiling
Using a quiet voice	Being patient	Tapping someone's shoulder repeatedly	

Good Friend	Not a Good Friend

Staying on Topic

Practice staying on topic. It is important to keep the topic in mind when having a conversation with others. Use the visual aid on the following page to practice staying on topic during your session. Cut out the arrow and practice having a conversation with a selected topic. Allow the client to decide if the comments made were "On Topic" or "Off Topic" and place the arrow where it belongs on the circle.

You should guide the conversation and interject off-topic comments and see if the client is able to identify them. After giving an off-topic comment, provide an on-topic comment to model expected skills. Discuss ways to stay on topic when talking with teachers, family or friends. The visual aid can be given to the caregiver to practice conversation skills at home.

Staying on Topic

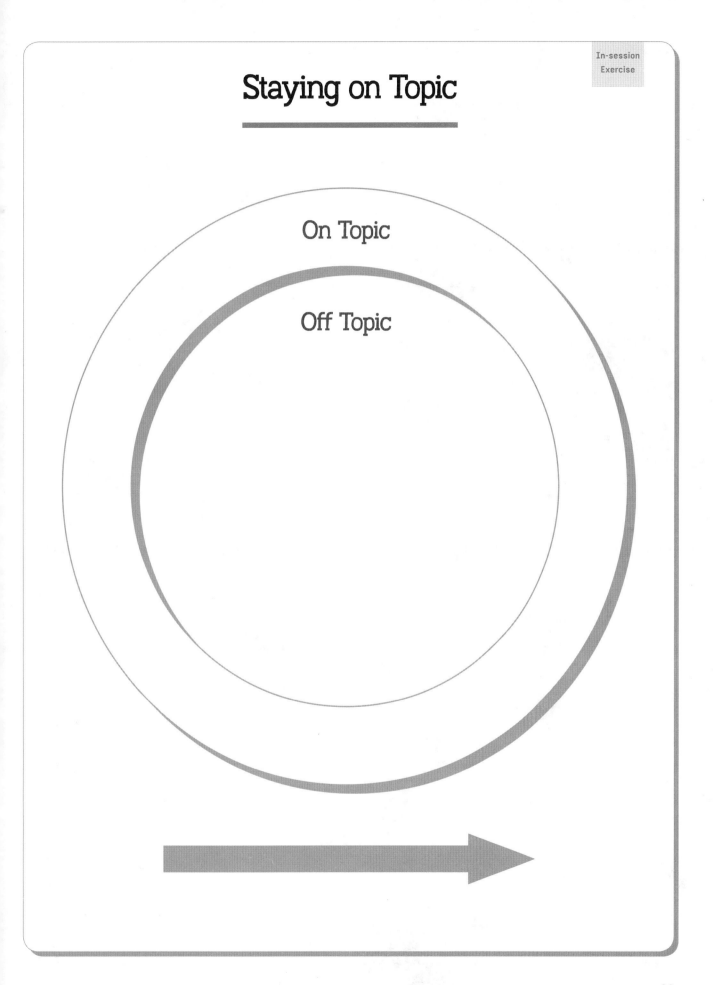

On Topic

Off Topic

Boundaries

It is important to understand personal boundaries and safety when talking to others. This activity highlights topics of conversation that are appropriate with each type of person and topics of conversation that are not appropriate.

	Things I Can Talk About	Things I Shouldn't Talk About
Family members		
Friends		
Teachers, other people who work at my school		
Community members (e.g., minister, coach, doctor, nurse)		
Authority figures (e.g., police officer, security guard)		
Strangers (e.g., met in person, met over the internet)		

How Big Is My Problem?

When problems occur at home or in school they can feel earth shattering. However, rarely are problems as bad as they seem. In moments of panic, it may be difficult for the client to put a problem into perspective. This activity helps clients create an anchor chart, in their own words, to help judge the severity of the problem and how to solve the problem. During the session, work with the client to brainstorm examples of minor, medium and major problems. Also allow the client to list a course of action for each level of problem. If needed, prompt clients with questions like; How can you solve this level of problem? Or: When do you need to seek assistance from others? This activity can be used in ongoing sessions and outside of the therapy to address real-life problems as they occur.

Major Problem! I Need Help!

Medium Problem

Small Problem

Does My Reaction Match My Problem?

Rate Your Problem: 1 (small)-10 (major) _____

_____

Describe Your Problem: _____

_____

Rate Your Reaction: 1 (small)-10 (major) _____

_____

Describe Your Reaction: _____

_____

Does Your Reaction Match Your Problem? _____

_____

Estimating Time

Time management is an important skill, particularly for children with attention deficits. This activity aims at helping children become more mindful of time. Have the child estimate the amount of time needed to complete the tasks below. Then, have the child complete the task and record the actual time. Discuss the child's accuracy in determining the amount of time needed to complete each task. Modify as needed or add additional activities to meet the needs of your child.

Materials Needed: Stopwatch.

Activity	Estimated Time to Complete Activity	Actual Time to Complete Activity
25 jumping jacks		
Walk around the room 2 times		
Say the alphabet (forward or backwards)		
Touch your shoulders then toes 10 times		
Walk to the nearest door and back to your seat 3 times		

Goal Setting Worksheet

Goal: What do I want to accomplish?

1. What is a reasonable amount of time to accomplish my goal?

2. What resources do I need to accomplish my goal? (e.g., parent support, therapist support, money, materials, training)

3. What steps do I need to take to accomplish my goal?

	Est. Time Required	Completed
Step 1:	_____	☐
Step 2:	_____	☐
Step 3:	_____	☐
Step 4:	_____	☐
Step 5:	_____	☐

Visualization of Distant Rewards

What is your long-term goal? _____

_____

_____

What steps need to be taken? _____

_____

_____

What setbacks may occur (e.g., mental, physical)? _____

_____

_____

What support do you need to be successful? _____

_____

_____

What are the long-term rewards? _____

_____

_____

Attention Regulator

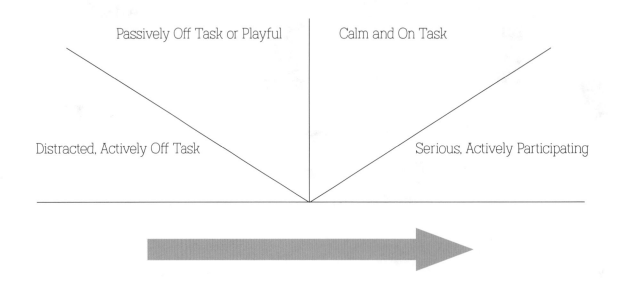

Cut out the arrow and attach it to the attention regulator to help the client recognize their behavior. The regulator can be used in future sessions as a visual reminder of expected behavior.

Describe what each attention state looks like and sounds like.

1. Serious, Actively Participating

Looks Like: _____

Sounds Like: _____

2. Calm and On Task

Looks Like: _____

Sounds Like: _____

3. Passively Off Task or Playful

Looks Like: _____

Sounds Like: _____

4. Distracted, Actively Off Task

Looks Like: _____

Sounds Like: _____

Action Regulator

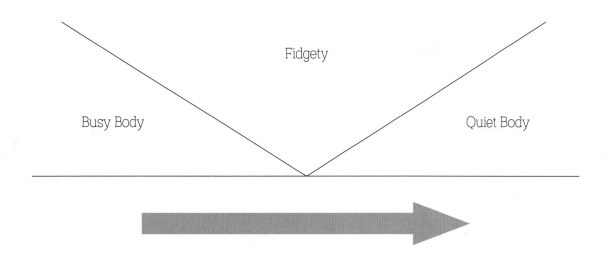

Cut out the arrow and attach it to the action regulator to help the client recognize their behavior. The regulator can be used in future sessions as a visual reminder of expected behavior.

Describe what each action state looks like and sounds like.

1. Quiet Body

Looks Like: _____

Impacts Client: _____

Impacts Others: _____

2. Fidgety

Looks Like: _____

Impacts Client: _____

Impacts Others: _____

3. Busy Body

Looks Like: _____

Impacts Client: _____

Impacts Others: _____

Stop and Think! Managing Impulsivity

Identify a time when you acted impulsively (e.g., talking to a parent or friend, completing work). In the chart that follows, think about the situation and the outcomes if you had stopped and thought about your response compared to when you acted impulsively.

Behavior or Situation: _____

	Stop and Think About It	Act on Impulse
What will you say?		
What are your actions?		
How do you feel?		
How will others react?		

Breaking It Down

Think of a task you need help completing. Break this task down into individual steps and draw or write a short description of each step in the boxes below, using one box per step. As you finish a step, make a mark on each square to help you stay focused on the task at hand.

Were you able to conceptualize chunking a large task into smaller steps?

What do you usually forget or skip? What consequences follow?

Cues on Cards

Work with the child to identify situations in which distractibility causes the most problems (e.g., settling into class, starting homework). Use an index card or the cards below to identify tips or "cues" to help the child be more successful at these tasks. The child may carry these cards in their pocket and review them before beginning these challenging tasks.

Starting Class

1. Stretch or shake out and take a seat.
2. Get out necessary books and pen.
3. Stay seated.
4. Raise hand before participating.
5. Repeat stretching or squeezing a stress ball as needed.
6. Imagine a quiet place and focus on learning.

Starting Homework

1. Set up quiet homework space with necessary books and pens/pencils.
2. Wear headphones if needed.
3. Choose which homework task to do first.
4. Take breaks to move or get a drink every 15 min. (Set timer if needed.)
5. Review homework to be sure all tasks are completed.
6. Place homework in backpack.

What are the identified problem tasks?

Was the child able to conceptualize the smaller steps needed to be successful in the larger task?

Were you helpful in offering support as the child thought through this activity?

Routinely check in with child to see if these cards are being used and are helpful.

Cognitive Flexibility

Learning to shift gears can be a challenging task for clients with weaknesses in attention and inhibition. This quick activity is to help children practice listening to directions, work accurately and be flexible when directions change. This activity can be used within a session or as a homework assignment. You or the parent will need two copies of the client page. For the first round, you or the caregiver should read the first set of directions stated below. Record the time it takes to complete the first round. During the second round, the directions will change, forcing the client to be more flexible in their thinking. Record the time it takes to complete this round. After the rounds are complete, review the time and accuracy with the client. Which task was easier for the client? How did it feel when the client was asked to complete the task in a different way? Did they use any strategies to help them when the directions were changed?

First Round: For each circle, draw a circle inside of the circle. For each square, draw a square inside the square. For each triangle draw a triangle inside of it. For each plus sign draw a plus sign inside of it.

Second Round: For each circle, draw a square inside of the circle. For each square, draw a circle inside. For each triangle, draw a plus sign inside, and for each plus sign, draw a triangle inside.

Cognitive Flexibility

Time the child to see how fast they can complete the exercise.

Calm Down Bingo

This version of bingo is a great way to practice attending to two step directions and "get the wiggles out." You the caregiver or client can use the game to introduce different, short movement breaks in a fun setting with the idea that the client can use the movement ideas when they are needed at home or school.

Write the letters on separate pieces of paper. Place then in a hat and have the child draw two letters. Using the worksheet on page 80, call out the letters and have the child perform the correlating task (e.g., A, D = 5 push-ups)

Calm Down Bingo

	C	A	L	M
D	20 big forward arm circles	5 push-ups	Hop on right foot 15 times	10 jumping jacks
O	Touch your head, shoulders, knees, and toes 5 times	5 deep breaths, like you were blowing up a balloon	Hands on waist, and twist for 20 seconds	Pretend to blow out 5 birthday candles
W	Move your right hand up and down and your left hand side to side at the same time 5 times	Hands over your head, and touch your toes 10 times	March in place for 20 seconds	20 big backward arm circles
N	10 deep breaths	10 wall push-ups	20 small arm circles	High knees in place 20 times

Animal Break Ladder

Take a quick movement break to help the child refocus and release energy. Follow the progression from quiet to louder back down to quiet. Compare how these creatures move. Who is the loudest? Who is the quietest? Which one do you relate to the most? Have the client take three deep breaths and return to work.

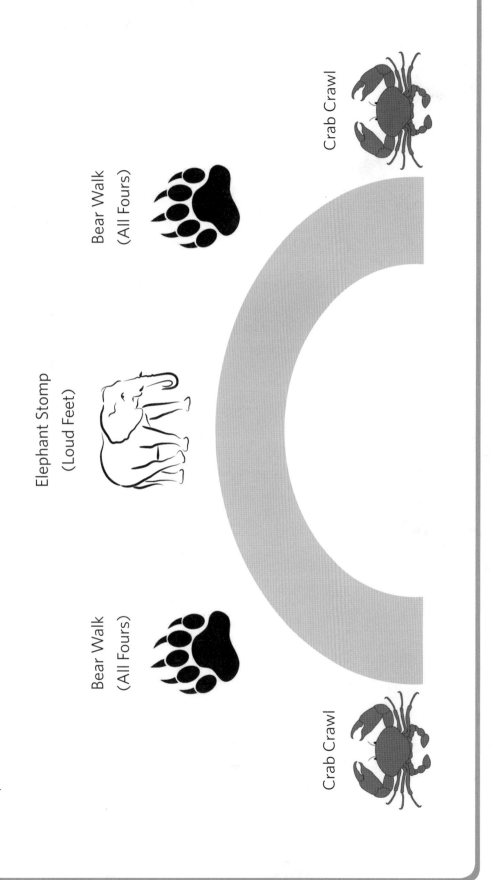

Crab Crawl

Bear Walk
(All Fours)

Elephant Stomp
(Loud Feet)

Bear Walk
(All Fours)

Crab Crawl

Whole-Body Games

Simple childhood games can be used to help children release physical energy and regain focus.

Red Light, Green Light

Have the child move from one side of the room to the other or down the hallway. *Green light* means go; *red light* means stop.

Statue

Tell the child to make a pose like a statue. Use a timer to see how long they can hold the pose.

Shake It Out!

Play a song for the child to dance to and stop it intermittently. When the music stops, the child should stop dancing.

Healthy Plate

The Healthy Plate exercise includes an image of a plate (page 82). Begin by discussing with the child (and caregiver) examples of healthy eating and balanced diet compared to unhealthy food choices. Then, instruct the client to fill the plate with drawings or magazine image cut-outs of healthy foods.

Consider making a copy of this plate and repeating this exercise to include healthy behaviors. Ask the client to identify healthy behaviors or actions and then fill the second plate with drawings or magazine image cut-outs of healthy actions. Some of these might include sleep, exercise, or healthy relationships.

After completion of this exercise, discuss with the child (and caregiver) the importance of healthy choices and how they can effect mood, behavior, and overall well-being. Ask the client to identify if it felt easy or challenging to identify healthy versus unhealthy. Engage in discussion about times when the client makes healthy versus unhealthy choices and the differences he/she feels after these choices.

Healthy Plate

Exercise Routine

Daily exercise is important for physical and mental health. What type of activity do you enjoy? What activities fit in your schedule? Indicate what type of physical activity you will do, and include it in your daily schedule. Keep track of your exercise and also take note of how you felt before, during, and after exercising. What exercises are more effective in helping you focus?

Day	Type of Activity	Time of Day	Amount of Time	How Do You Feel Before, During, and After Exercising?

Time for Bed

The child and caregiver should work together to break down the bedtime routine into steps. Write each step below and fill in the appropriate time of night next to it to help ensure a healthy bedtime routine.

Example:

1. Shower 6:45
2. Pajamas 7:10
3. Brush hair and teeth 7:15
4. Go to bathroom 7:20
5. Read 7:25
6. In and deep breathing 7:40

Is the current bedtime and bedtime routine appropriate? Is there anything that needs to be added to the bedtime routine to assist with child and caregiver bonding?

Step: Time:

1. _____   [ ]

2. _____   [ ]

3. _____   [ ]

4. _____   [ ]

5. _____   [ ]

6. _____   [ ]

Positive Self-Reflection Log

Each night, reflect on a positive way that you maintained attention or controlled your impulses that day.

DAY 1 _____

DAY 2 _____

DAY 3 _____

DAY 4 _____

DAY 5 _____

DAY 6 _____

DAY 7 _____

Positive Imagery Practice:
In Control and Focused

What events are the most challenging for you? Close your eyes and imagine the event as if it were occurring now; however, instead of being uncomfortable, you are now in control. What does this look like? How does this feel? What will be the outcome of being in control of your behavior?

Describe your feelings:

_____

_____

Describe
the event:

_____

_____

_____

_____

Describe your thoughts:

_____

_____

Describe the potential outcomes:

_____

_____

Look at What I Accomplished

Making lists is a life skill that is helpful for remembering all that needs to be done, particularly for people who have difficulty with time management and organization. Add this list to your daily agenda or journal to help keep focused on your accomplishments and goals.

My Long-Term Goal: _____

_____

_____

_____

_____

_____

_____

_____

What I Have Accomplished So Far:_____

_____

_____

_____

_____

_____

_____

_____

_____

Autism Spectrum Disorder

A utism is a spectrum disorder, meaning that clients may present with a range of strengths and weaknesses in the areas of social functioning, language, and stereotypical behavior, requiring a tailoring of treatment. This section targets areas of need including communication, social functioning, and sensory integration using a whole brain approach. Activities include a variety of worksheets, games and graphic organizers to help make sense of a world that can be overwhelming at times.

Cognitive skills covered in this section provide social scripts from self-advocacy, embracing change and becoming aware of sensory sensitivities that may impact daily living. Relationship-building activities allow clients to explore perspective taking, expressing emotion, and developing mindfulness in communication. Competency-building activities are aimed at helping children identify triggers to anxiety, understand perseveration behaviors and how these behaviors impact their attention, and practice coping skills in order to handle difficult situations. Furthermore, sensory integration is addressed through exploring personal tolerances to sensory experiences, understanding how sensory reactions impact thinking and functioning, and developing coping plans to mitigate the reactions.

Remember, patience is crucial when working with children who have unique, often rigid thinking patterns. The goal is to use the activities to guide the child to accept change in thinking patterns. Certain skills can be completed quickly, while others need continuous practice and reinforcement. Pairing activities with real-life scenarios can help facilitate the transferring of skills to outside of the therapeutic environment.

Allow Me to Introduce Myself

Establishing new relationships can be difficult especially for individuals with social deficits. The fear of the unknown or simple misunderstanding of social cues can make talking with someone new very overwhelming. This activity was designed to help build social confidence in new social settings by using a social script.

Social scripts provide a way for children to advocate for themselves and help start a conversation. Have the client try to complete the script in session and practice delivering the script to you or the caregiver. Identify who and where the client might use a script like this. Additional activities could include modifying the script to address needs in different settings (e.g., school, after school activities, friends, etc.).

Allow Me to Introduce Myself

My name is _____.

I am _____ years old. I am unique and intelligent.

I think differently than others at times, so please be patient.

I prefer to communicate by _____.

I am very good at _____.

My favorite thing(s) to do is/are _____.

I am interested in learning about _____.

It is difficult for me to _____.

At times, I get distracted by _____.

When I get upset, I tend to _____.

I learn best when _____

_____.

I would like help with _____.

I look forward to being part of _____.

Thank you for listening.

Conversation Map

Having a conversation with another person can be a challenging situation. A conversation has multiple stages. Use the map below to help navigate through each step of a conversation. Describe what you should say and what you should do with your body. Finally, draw a symbol or find an image to help illustrate or remind you of the step.

Steps	What do you say or do?	What do you do with your body?	Symbol
Greeting	"Hello"	Put your hand out, good eye contact	
Starting a conversation	"How are you?" "Guess what happened?"		
Conversation	Taking turns with individual Ask questions that are on topic Be brief and give important details		
Farewell	Say "goodbye"		

Conversation Toolkit

For each area, list ways to initiate a conversation and keep it going. List words or phrases that you might say and describe how your body should look. These tools can be used if you get stuck trying to communicate with others.

Greeting	Giving a Compliment	Gaining Someone's Attention

Asking Questions	Giving Precise Answers	Farewell

Flexible vs. Rigid Thinking

Flexible thinking occurs when you are able to adapt to changes in your environment. Rigid thinking occurs when you are not able to accept change and become stuck when presented with a challenge. In the following shapes, list items that are flexible (e.g., dough, string) or rigid (e.g., rock, pencil). Then brainstorm ways that thinking can be flexible (e.g., telling someone they hurt your feelings when you are upset, listening to others' opinions even if you disagree) or rigid (e.g., yelling at someone when upset, not listening to others).

Flexible
Objects

Rigid Objects

Flexible
Thinking

Rigid Thinking

Dealing with Detours

What do you do when your daily routine is changed? Do you have a backup plan? Preparing yourself for change can help you become more flexible. Describe your daily routine and then brainstorm ways you can adjust if your schedule changes.

Daily Routine	Backup Plan

Embracing Change

Change is constant in our lives. Daily routines can be altered by changes that are sometimes out of our control. While change can bring uncertainty, having a plan in place can help reduce the stress typically associated with change. Complete the responses for the scenarios below and then use them to address a specific change occurring in your life.

Practice Changing

	Minor Change (e.g., change in schedule—no art class today)	**Moderate Change** (e.g., having a new teacher)	**Major Change** (e.g., moving to a new house)
How do you feel?			
How do you stay in control?			
What could make this easier?			
Name something positive that can occur due to accepting this change.			

Real Life Change

What is changing?	
How do you feel?	
How do you stay in control?	
What could make this easier?	
Name something positive that can occur due to accepting this change.	

Sensory Profile

People have different levels of tolerance to their senses. It is important to gain awareness of your sensitivities so you can be proactive in reducing how they affect you. For instance, if loud noises bother you, you can use noise-canceling headphones in loud places. Use this chart to indicate what bothers you, the most common places where sensory overload may happen, and how to handle it.

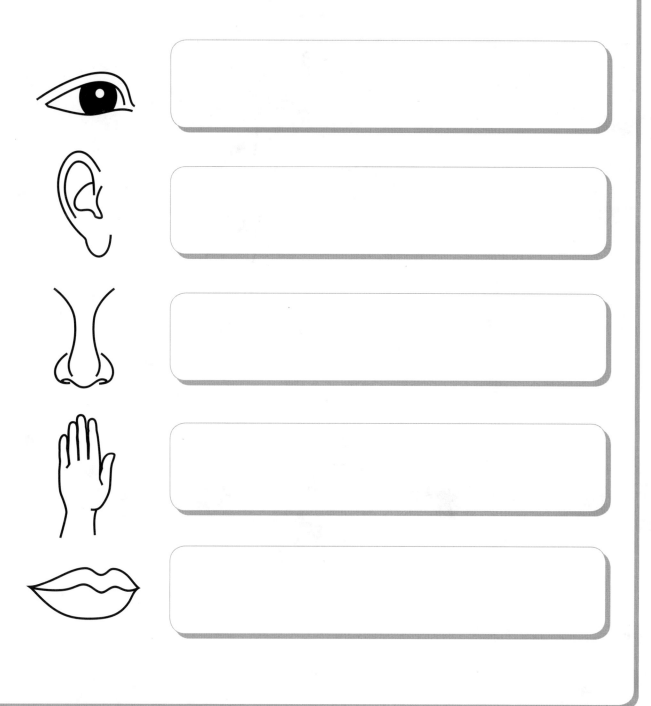

Sensory Awareness

Think of a sensory experience that causes discomfort. Label that sensory experience to the left of the figure and write the impact or feeling to the right. Then determine where in your body you experience that feeling. Use colors, shapes, and/or imagery to show how that feeling feels inside your body. Discuss ways that your discomfort can be reduced when faced with these sensory experiences.

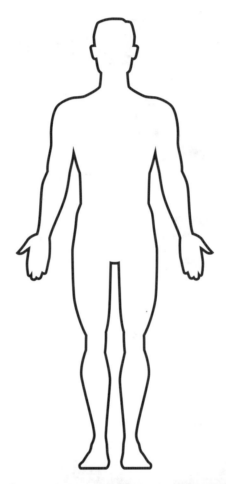

Sensory Experience	Impact	What can I do to reduce the impact?

Sensory Escape

Where do you go and what do you do when presented with uncomfortable sensory information? Are your reactions appropriate? What do you do to stay in control? In the following chart, list sensory experiences that are troublesome. Write your typical response, positive or negative. Then brainstorm another, healthier approach to dealing with the sensory input in the future.

Sensory Experience	Typical Reaction	Alternative Approach
Example: Peers coughing or making noises when trying to complete work.	Example: Tell them to stop making noise, get frustrated and not complete work.	Example: Use headphones, ask to sit in another area in the room.

Perspective Taking

What did you say? In this activity, think about recent interactions with others. In the left bubbles, write what you said. In the right bubbles, indicate how others perceived your words. Were they kind words, helpful words, or negative words? Did you show interest in other ideas or thoughts, or stay on one topic? What kind of feedback did you get from others?

What I Said	What Others Might Think

Looking at All Sides

Our words and actions are multidimensional. They can impact people around us in positive or negative ways. Stepping back and looking at the impact of our actions can be helpful. You know how it felt to help someone or to yell at someone, but how did that affect others around you? In the following chart, list some positive and negative actions you've done. List what those actions looked like and the impact they had on others.

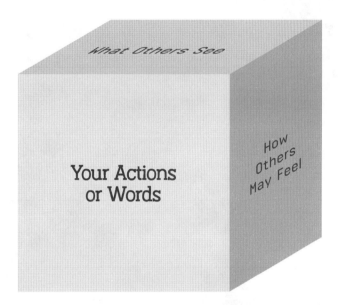

Positive			Negative		
Actions/Words	What Others See	How Others May Feel	Actions/Words	What Others See	How Others May Feel

Common Ground

Homework time! Good conversation occurs when both parties are talking about common interests. Ask a family member and a friend about their interests. Then compare their interests with yours. What do you have in common? If your interests are different, ask a question to find about more about one of the other person's interests. Write the results below.

Interview a Family Member

Family Member's Name: _____

What are your interests? _____

_____

_____

What do we have in common? _____

_____

_____

*Additional Comments*_____

_____

Interview a Friend

Friend's Name: _____

What are your interests? _____

_____

_____

What do we have in common? _____

_____

_____

*Additional Comments*_____

_____

Emotions Cheat Sheet

Build a quick reference to expand your emotional vocabulary. For the emotions listed below, draw in the circle what a person having that emotion would look like, then underneath, describe what each emotion looks and feels like. To aid with the drawings, search for faces on the Internet or in magazines that show how facial expressions differ with different emotions.

| Happy | Sad | Worried | Tired | Excited |

| Angry | Annoyed | Mad | Silly | Stressed |

Understanding Emotions

For each emotion in the circle, write what it looks and sounds like. In the adjoining rectangles, write about a situation in which you experienced the emotion and then try and recall a time when others may have felt the emotion. You may use magazines or computer images of others to help provide a visual representation of each emotion.

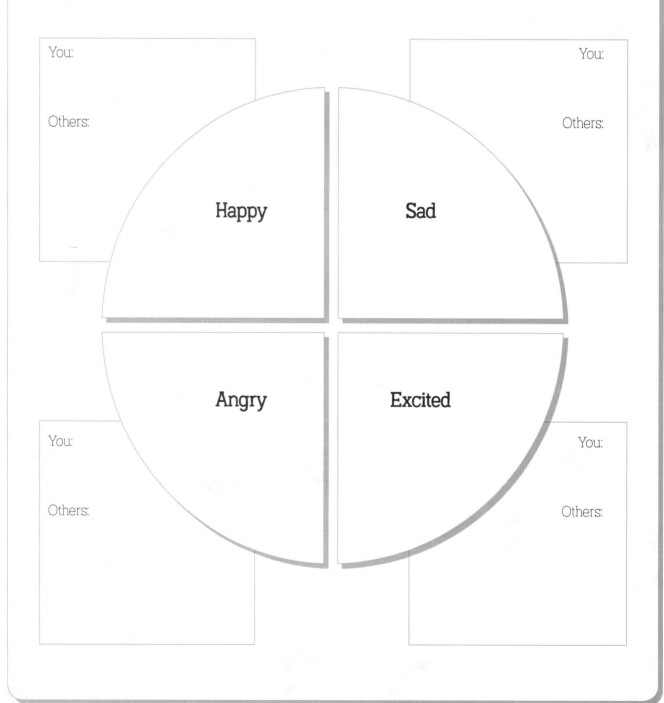

You:

Others:

You:

Others:

Happy

Sad

Angry

Excited

You:

Others:

You:

Others:

What's My Emotional Temperature?

EXPLOSIVE

How does it feel? _____

What do I do? _____

How do I look? _____

What can other people do? _____

AGITATED

How does it feel? _____

What do I do? _____

How do I look? _____

What can other people do? _____

EXCITED

How does it feel? _____

What do I do? _____

How do I look? _____

What can other people do? _____

CALM

How does it feel? _____

What do I do? _____

How do I look? _____

What can other people do? _____

Mindful Communication

In the next potentially tense conversation with someone you know well, practice mindfulness and observe the other person's physical and verbal behavior. Take note of how they hold their body, their facial expressions, the tone of their voice, and their interactions with the environment around them. Notice your own verbal or physical behavior during the interaction. Consider your feelings and needs in the interaction and how you could express them in a way that maintains the relationship. If you find anything hard to read or understand, ask clarifying questions. Consider the following scenario:

Josh went to school and walked into the classroom. Josh put his things in his cubby and sat at his desk, eating his breakfast and working on his morning school work. Another student and Josh's best friend, Mary, walked into class right after he did. Mary looked upset, as if she had been crying. This was not like Mary, as Mary always had a smile on her face. Mary immediately went to the teacher for help. Mary started crying, yelling, and throwing things around the classroom. The teacher was having a hard time calming Mary down. Josh came over to the teacher and Mary to see if he could help. Mary seemed to calm down, with Josh's help. Mary explained that her mom woke up late and was unable to stop for breakfast, like she had promised the night before. Josh apologized and offered to share his breakfast and snack with Mary. Mary appeared more calm, as she smiled and thanked Josh for sharing and helping her calm down.

In this scenario, Josh was aware of Mary's verbal and nonverbal behavior. He observed that Mary appeared angry and asked her if he could help make her feel better. Josh acknowledged Mary's feelings and offered an alternative to her behavior. Following are some open-ended questions (questions that can't be answered with a simple "yes" or "no") that may help create a safe environment and constructive conversation in uncomfortable situations with loved ones.

1. How are you feeling?

2. How can I help?

3. You seem to feel _____. Is this an accurate perception of your feelings?

4. I am hearing you say _____. Is that right?

5. How are things between us?

6. How are we doing?

7. Are we okay?

8. I noticed _____. Is there anything you need to talk about?

9. How can I help you feel better about _____?

10. Are you doing okay?

"I" Statement 101

Discussing sensitive and difficult topics with people that we care about can become confusing with emotions. Sometimes we feel unheard or blamed for doing something we didn't do. The purpose of "I" statements is to communicate your feelings and needs in an assertive manner and reduce blame and accusations toward others. "You" statements may make the listener feel criticized and defensive and less likely to engage thoughtfully with you. You can use "I" statements when you are feeling hurt, sad, anxious, angry, and happy. It is important to practice using positive "I" statements during low stress encounters to prepare for more stressful interactions. "I" statements typically follow a set pattern beginning with saying "I" and how you feel. Then express what occurred that provoked your feelings. Finish with saying what it was about the behavior that hurt your feelings, and say what you would prefer and/or offer a suggestion.

Examples:

Teacher: "I feel angry when you call on me in class and I don't want to be called on. It makes me feel like you are picking on me. I would like for you to only call on me when I raise my hand."

Friend: "I feel sad when you don't play with me at recess because I look forward to playing on the play set. I would like for you to let me know when you don't want to play, instead of ignoring me."

Parent: "I feel worried when you don't say "bye" to me in the morning before you leave for work, because I feel that you are mad at me. I would like for you to always say "bye" to me, even if it wakes me up in the morning."

I feel _____

When _____

Because _____

What I need/want is _____

_____

_____

_____

Think about a recent or upcoming situation with a teacher, friend, or parent where you need to communicate your thoughts and feelings. Use the script to the left to effectively communicate your needs in a positive manner.

"I" Statements vs. "You" Statements

Read the following statements and consider your reactions if they were said to you by a friend or family member. Consider how the statements would make your friends and family members feel. Write down your thoughts in the chart. In the last column, change what was said to minimize blame and communicate what you mean clearly with "I" statements.

"You" Statement	How Do They Make You Feel? How Would They Make Others Feel?	"I" Statement
You never listen to me.		
You make me so angry.		
Why do you always yell at me?		
You're mean.		
You never pick me first.		
You don't love me.		
You hate me.		
You always say mean things to me.		
You don't do anything right.		
Why do you make things so hard for me?		
Why do you even bother?		

Is it an Emergency?

Review the six levels of problems and the examples given, then brainstorm two other possible problems for each level and write them on the chart.

EMERGENCY

You definitely need help from an adult

- A building is on fire
- Someone is hurt and needs to go to the hospital
- _____
- _____

GIGANTIC PROBLEM

You can make a change with a lot of help

- You are lost
- You hit or kicked someone
- _____
- _____

BIG PROBLEM

You can make a change with some more help

- Someone is being mean to you
- You aren't doing well in a class
- _____
- _____

MEDIUM PROBLEM

You can make a change with some help

- You feel sick, tired, or hungry
- Someone is bothering you
- _____
- _____

PROBLEM

You can make a change with a little help

- You did not get your way
- You did not win a game
- _____
- _____

GLITCH

You can fix the problem yourself

- You need to clean up your work area
- You forgot your homework
- _____
- _____

Expected vs. Unexpected

Expected behaviors are those that are predictable, socially acceptable, and help us do our best. Unexpected behaviors can deter our progress and cause others to view us differently. Understanding sets of acceptable behaviors can help us be prepared and successful. For each setting, write examples of expected and unexpected behaviors. Are there similar expected behaviors among the settings? Use the "Behavior Bank" on the next page or think of your own.

Home

Expected Behaviors	Unexpected Behaviors

School

Expected Behaviors	Unexpected Behaviors

Friendship

Expected Behaviors	Unexpected Behaviors

Behavior Bank

Saying hello to friends	Pushing classmates	Listening to teacher
Yelling out in class	Finishing your work	Taking turns
Looking at others when they are talking to you	Sitting in assigned area	Saying mean things
Following rules	Helping with chores	Cleaning up your area
Laughing at a mistake	Sharing	Raising your hand
Using manners	Covering your ears when someone is talking	Standing in someone's space
Walking in the hallway		

Examining Expectations

Compare expectations that you have for others with what is expected of you. Note differences among family, friends, and teachers.

What behaviors do you expect from others?

Parents/Caregivers	Teachers	Friends
(e.g., listen, care for me)	(e.g., instruct me, be patient)	(e.g., include me, play my favorite game)

What behaviors do others expect from you?

Parents/Caregivers	Teachers	Friends
(e.g., follow rules, do chores)	(e.g., follow rules, do chores)	(e.g., play games, talk)

My Personal Bubble

Your personal bubble is the invisible space around your body. When you are talking with other people, there are rules for how close or far away you should stand, depending on how well you know them. In the diagram below, fill in names of friends, family, and community members that you think fit into each zone. How does it make you feel to have people stand in each zone?

Intimate
Family and closest friends
Almost able to touch

Personal
People you know well
Arm's distance apart

Social
People you don't know very well
A few feet apart

Public
People giving a speech or talking in a group
Over four feet apart

Control My Volume

Personal volume is the loudness or softness of a speaking voice. It is important to think about volume, because if your voice is too quiet or too loud it can make others feel uncomfortable.

Look at the list of situations below. Check the box in the column that shows the correct volume of voice that should be used for each situation.

Situation	Soft	Normal	Loud
Working with a partner in class	❑	❑	❑
Studying in the library	❑	❑	❑
Cheering at a sports game	❑	❑	❑
Playing inside	❑	❑	❑
Playing outside	❑	❑	❑
When someone is sleeping	❑	❑	❑
Talking on the phone	❑	❑	❑
Shopping at the supermarket	❑	❑	❑
Watching a movie	❑	❑	❑
Riding on a bus	❑	❑	❑
Talking at lunchtime	❑	❑	❑

Pick three of the situations listed above and explain why you chose the volume level you did.

1. Situation: _____

   Why: _____

2. Situation: _____

   Why: _____

3. Situation: _____

   Why: _____

Appropriate Touching

Touching can be a form of communication. For example, if someone is patted on the back, it usually shows that they have done a good job. However, if they are slapped, it might mean that they have made someone angry.

Read through the examples of touching listed below. Decide if the type of touching was appropriate or inappropriate. If you mark something as appropriate, write with whom you might use that type of touching.

	Appropriate	Inappropriate	Who can I touch in this way?
Giving someone a high five	❑	❑	
Jumping on someone	❑	❑	
Slapping any part of another person's body	❑	❑	
Putting arm around someone	❑	❑	
Kicking	❑	❑	
Pinching someone	❑	❑	
Holding hands	❑	❑	

Perseveration Log

Use this log daily to note the child's perseverating behaviors and frequency to help track and measure how often these behaviors occur.

TIME (e.g., 7–7:15 AM)	BEHAVIOR (e.g., repeating a question)	REASONS FOR BEHAVIOR (e.g., feeling anxious about an upcoming event)

Perseveration Information

Complete the questions below to gather more information about perseverating behaviors. This activity may be completed in session and at home. Use this activity during or after an episode of perseveration to help devise a plan for moving forward. Repeat the exercise as needed and highlight the pattern, triggers, and helpful strategies.

What is the perseverating behavior?

What is the feeling that causes this behavior? (e.g., stress, worry, fear ...)

What does the client gain from this behavior? How is this behavior soothing?

List a healthier alternative behavior/ activity that will provide the same comfort.

When should there be a stopping point?

How are others responding/reacting to this behavior?

Perseveration Action Plan

The Perseveration Plan worksheet is helpful in gathering information about the client's cycle of perseveration. Identify any common themes or feelings. Use this information to help devise a plan for recognizing challenging perseverations and replacing unhealthy thoughts with healthy alternatives. Discuss any stimulus or situations that might need to be avoided to help reduce stress or other unpleasant feelings that result in perseverating behaviors.

During the session, introduce the topic of perseveration with the client and help the client define behavior in observable terms (e.g. what does it look like, sound like, etc.). Do this exercise in session with the client to be sure of understanding. Consider making additional copies of this exercise to send home with the client. Ask client and caregiver to identify any additional perseveration behaviors over the next week and fill out a worksheet each time a new preservation behavior is experienced. Review the worksheet at next session and as often as needed to measure progress.

Perseveration Action Plan

Do you experience repeating or perseverative thoughts that get you off task? Use this worksheet to help identify preservative behaviors that interrupt or distract you. Review with your therapist and caregiver to reflect on how these behaviors look and feel. Then discuss how these behaviors may look and feel to others around you.

What am I repeatedly doing?

(e.g., asking a question, repeating a phrase, repeating a thought, stuck on a feeling, banging, pacing)

What feeling do I have?

(e.g., anger, sadness, fear, frustration, worry)

Where do I experience this feeling inside my body?

(e.g., belly, back, neck, shoulders, face, hands, feet)

How are others reacting to me?

(e.g., answering my questions, asking me to stop, placing their hands on my body, wrapping me in a hug, yelling at me, ignoring me)

What feelings do others have about this behavior?

(e.g., worry, frustration, anger, happiness, disappointment, fear, annoyance)

How long and how often have I been doing this behavior?

(e.g., for how many minutes, how many times repeated?)

Cool Down Checklist

Doing things that are pleasurable and make you feel good can help you relax. It is helpful to engage in these types of activities on a regular, or even daily, basis. Exercise is especially important because it has been linked with the release of endorphins, which leads to feeling better and more relaxed.

Check the activities you're willing to do, and then add any other activities you can think of.

❏ Lift weights	❏ Go jogging	❏ Stretch your muscles	❏ Ride your bike
❏ Talk to a friend on the phone	❏ Do yoga	❏ Go for a swim	❏ Go hiking
❏ Go outside and watch the clouds	❏ Go rock climbing	❏ Go kayaking	❏ Play basketball
❏ Get a massage	❏ Get out of the house	❏ Go for a ride in the car	❏ Play with your pet
❏ Go bowling	❏ Visit a friend	❏ Play video games	❏ Cook your favorite food
❏ Watch a funny movie	❏ Meditate	❏ Do yard work, such as mowing	❏ Grow a garden
❏ Learn to knit or crochet	❏ Join a social club	❏ Play tennis	❏ Go shopping
❏ Listen to the radio or stream a radio station	❏ Watch TV	❏ Clean your room	❏ Write in a journal
❏	❏	❏	❏

Racetrack Breathing:

Warm Up or Cool Down

Warm Up (Before Doing an Activity)

1. Put your finger at the starting line. Take a deep breath in for six counts as you move your finger along the curve.

2. As your finger reaches the straightaway, breathe out for four counts.

3. Keep tracing and breathing until your body and mind are ready to work.

Cool Down (After Doing an Activity)

1. Put your finger at the starting line. Take a deep breath in for four counts as you move your finger along the curve.

2. As your finger reaches the straightaway, breathe out for four counts.

3. Keep tracing and breathing until your body and mind are calm.

Straightaway

Curve

Curve

Starting
Line

Straightaway

Visual Breathing

In the hexagon below write calming words or find calming images that will remind you to relax. Then practice your breathing. Use your finger to trace the hexagon shape. Put your finger on the starting point and begin by taking a deep breath in on a count of six. Then breathe out on a count of six. Keep tracing until your body and mind feel calm.

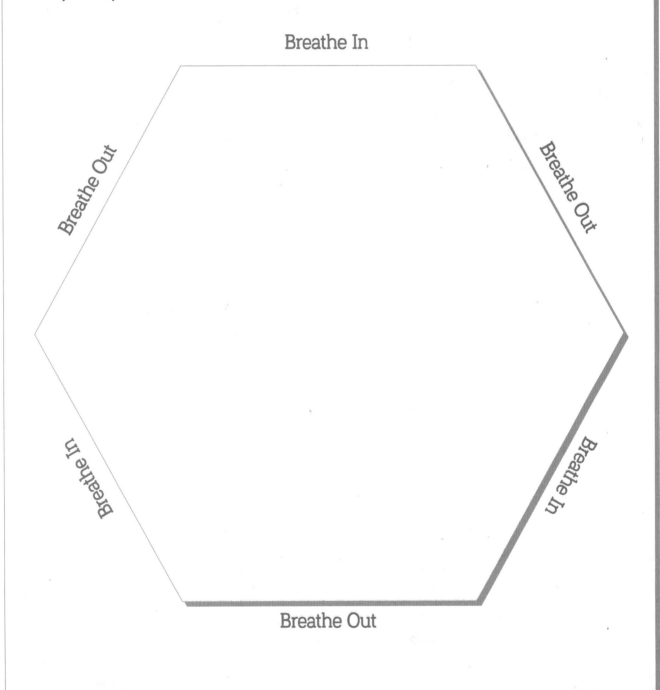

How Can I Help?

Read the following scenarios aloud. **Brainstorm** how you can help in each situation. **Review** your ideas and **act out** the scene with a partner using the solution you chose.

Set the Scene

1. Your father is making dinner, and you are sitting at the kitchen table.
   Dad says, "I need to get the table set and tell the family that dinner is ready."

   What can you say and do that will help in this situation?

   _____

   _____

   _____

2. **ACT IT OUT Reflection**

   Did my words and actions help my father?   **YES   NO**

   If the answer was **yes**, explain how you were helpful. _____

   If the answer was **no**, what should have you said or done? _____

Set the Scene

1. During free time, you notice that your teacher is cleaning up the classroom.
   Your teacher says, "There is so much to do!"

   What can you say and do that will help in this situation?

   _____

   _____

   _____

2. **ACT IT OUT Reflection**

   Did my words and actions help my teacher?   **YES   NO**

   If the answer was **yes**, explain how you were helpful. _____

   If the answer was **no**, what should have you said or done? _____

Set the Scene

1. You are getting home from the grocery store with your mother.
Mom says, "There are a lot of bags to carry inside."

What can you say and do that will help in this situation?

_____

_____

_____

2. ACT IT OUT Reflection

Did my words and actions help my mother?   **YES   NO**

If the answer was **yes**, explain how you were helpful. _____

_____

_____

_____

If the answer was **no**, what should have you said or done? _____

_____

_____

_____

I CAN Make a Choice

Fill in the blank squares with strategies that will help you when you are feeling nervous, scared, upset, or frustrated. The upper squares contain some ideas you could use. Leave this card where you can see it to help you remember strategies to remain calm.

Sit and count to 10.

Think about a safe place.

Give my teacher a break card.

What choice will make me feel better?

Ask for help.

Breathe in and out slowly.

Reaching Out for Help

Do you know when to ask for help? Some problems require the assistance of others, whereas you can solve others by yourself. Read through the problems listed below. Identify how big the problem is, who can help, and how to ask them if help is needed.

Problem	How Big Is the Problem?	Who Can Help Me?	How Do I Ask for Help?
The radio is too loud.			
You got lost on a walk.			
You lost an important paper for school.			
Your bike has a flat tire.			
You broke your pencil in class.			
There is a fire in the neighbor's house.			

Emotional Connection Game

1. Cut out the emotion cards below and place them in a bowl.
2. Pick one emotion card.
3. Act out the emotion.
4. Complete the following sentence using the emotion word on the card you picked.

I feel _____ when…

Cheerful	Confused	Embarrassed
Proud	Depressed	Nervous
Jealous	Lonely	Disappointed
Overwhelmed	Guilty	Shy

Find a Friend

Starting conversations can be difficult, but there is usually some common ground. The object of the game is to find as many things in common as you can with another person. For homework, interview a family member or friends. What do you have in common? What is different? What would you like to know more about? Remember to use good eye contact and respect personal space.

Question	Myself	Name
What is your favorite book?		
What is your favorite movie?		
Do you like pets?		
What is your favorite food?		
What is your favorite thing to do to relax?		
What is your favorite subject in school?		

Conversation Cube

Cut out the shape and fold and tape it to make a cube. Roll the cube and use the phrase or question you roll to practice having a conversation with someone. Remember to pay attention to your nonverbal behaviors like eye contact, posture, and personal space.

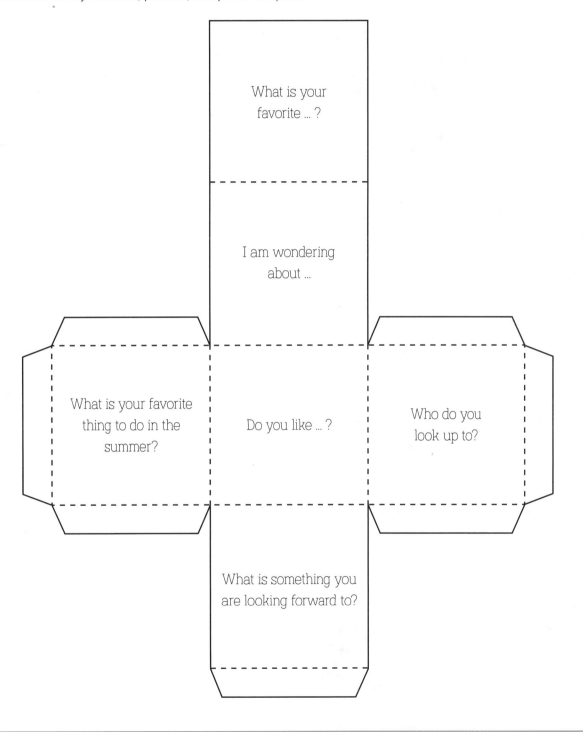

Conduct Disorder

The approach to identifying and improving the performance of students with disruptive, aggressive behaviors has undergone significant changes. We are better able to identify the symptomatology of multiple disruptive behavior disorders, including oppositional defiant disorder, conduct disorder, and intermittent explosive behavior disorder. The common characteristics of anger and aggressiveness often stem from a combination of biological, familial, and environmental factors; however, the disorders vary in severity and impact. The developmental course of disruptive behavior disorders is significant; for example, if the early expressions of oppositional defiant disorder are addressed, there is a lower probability that the more destructive behaviors related to conduct disorder will develop. The course of intermittent explosive disorder is separate from the other disorders but can have severe outcomes if symptoms are not treated.

Current treatment of conduct disorders is focused on improving the use of positive pro-social thoughts, feelings, relationships, and behaviors as an alternative to reducing negative behaviors. This section focuses attention on teaching specific skills that help children use reasoning to improve the accuracy of reading other individuals' emotional states and intent. This increases the child's ability to change their emotional arousal level to fit the situation and experience an appropriate level of emotional response to challenging social situations. Activities provide a way to maximize positive ways of addressing problems and help clients actively engage in pro-social behaviors. The aim is to help children evaluate and change their emotional experiences and expressions rather than be at the mercy of their thoughts and emotions.

Activities in this chapter may also be useful for clients with other diagnoses that have anger, irritability, and aggression as symptoms.

Getting to Know Your Anger

1. Describe a recent situation when you experienced difficulty controlling your anger. Remember to describe the what, where, and why of this situation. _____

   _____

   _____

   _____

2. Was there anything you could have changed about this situation to make it less anger provoking? Was there anything you could have changed to make it more peaceful (e.g., avoid the situation, ask for help)? _____

   _____

   _____

   _____

3. List the things you were not able to change about this situation. What didn't you have control over?

   _____

   _____

   _____

4. Describe a recent situation where you felt in control of your emotions or at ease. _____

   _____

   _____

5. Describe your thoughts regarding the peaceful situation. What were you thinking? What were you feeling? _____

   _____

   _____

6. When in an anger-provoking situation, if you were able to accept your thoughts and the situation for what they are, what would change for you? _____

   _____

   _____

   _____

Tackling Anger Mountain

Identify five events that make you angry, starting with an event that makes you feel irritable and ending with an event that makes you very mad. Identify how your body feels in those situations. Notice the change as your emotions change. List strategies you can use to calm down and gain control of your thoughts and feelings.

Intensity	Trigger	Body Feelings	Calm Down Strategies
1			
2			
3			
4			
5			

Weekly Anger Diary

Logging your feelings is a great way to understand triggers for your emotions, as well as how you respond to your feelings. Track your anger for a week. Do you notice any patterns? Do your feelings and actions match the size of the problem? How long does it take you to recover?

Date: _____   Time: _____

Trigger	
Actions	
Feelings	
Outcome	
Time it took to recover	

Date: _____   Time: _____

Trigger	
Actions	
Feelings	
Outcome	
Time it took to recover	

Date: _____   Time: _____

Trigger	
Actions	
Feelings	
Outcome	
Time it took to recover	

Date: _____   Time: _____

Trigger	
Actions	
Feelings	
Outcome	
Time it took to recover	

Times of Acting Out

On the following pages, you will find two worksheets that look very similar. The first is for the **client** to complete and the second is for the **caregiver**. Make as many copies as needed, and invite each individual to take this worksheet home to track times of acting out and other supporting information.

At the next session, review the completed worksheets. Discuss any discrepancies or differences in the details reported between the two perspectives. Encourage the child and caregiver to identify any relationships or patterns to acting-out behaviors. Observe if the outbursts seem to follow any mood, state, environmental cue or time of day. Notice if there are any verbal or nonverbal cues that present prior to the outburst behaviors.

After this discussion, move on to the third worksheet. Make note in the appropriate boxes of the identified cues or feeling states that precede the acting-out behaviors. In the adjacent box, make a note of how to prevent this. The prevention plan can include behaviors by both child and caregiver. Once this page is completed, invite the client and caregiver to take home this worksheet to review this prevention plan as needed.

Repeat this exercise as often as needed. Track changes and improvements in behaviors and note the prevention strategies that seem to best help the client avoid acting-out behaviors.

Times of Acting Out

Make daily notes on the time and intensity/description of acting-out behaviors. Use an intensity rating of 0 to 10, with 10 being most intense. In addition, make notes on any other information that was noticed prior to the acting-out behaviors.

Time of Day	Intensity Rating	Description	Additional Notes
7:30 AM	7	Yelled because my mom made me oatmeal instead of toast.	Slept through my alarm. Upset that my mom was rushing me to get ready.

Times of Acting Out

Make daily notes on the time and intensity/description of acting-out behaviors of the child in this log. Use an intensity rating of 0 to 10, with 10 being most intense. In addition, make notes on any other information that was noticed prior to the acting-out behaviors.

Time of Day	Intensity Rating	Description	Additional Notes
7:30 AM	7	Yelled at me for giving him the wrong breakfast.	Didn't want to get out of bed. Irritable.

Times of Acting Out:
Plan of Action

Make a list of the environmental cues and feeling states that preceded the acting out from the previous workbook page. Write a plan of action of what the client and the caregiver can do when these cues take place in the future to prevent acting out.

Cues/Feeling States Preceding Acting Out	Actions That May Prevent Acting Out

Going Back in Time

Describe the moment of distress and list any feelings/behaviors observed:

Going back in time, list all events leading up to the distressed mood:

1. _____

2. _____

3. _____

4. _____

5. _____

Recognizing Emotional Limits

Emotional responses to situations are unique to the individual. Different situations can elicit different emotions among different people. This activity is designed to help you recognize what situations trigger different emotions and where your emotional limits lie. In the boxes below, list two examples of what makes you feel this emotion.

OUTRAGED

1.

2.

ANGRY

1.

2.

FRUSTRATED

1.

2.

ANNOYED

1.

2.

CALM

1.

2.

Body Reactions

People respond to feelings of anger in different ways. Think about a time when you were upset or angry. How did your body react? Write a few words to describe your feelings and then color or draw on the body to show where you experienced the feelings.

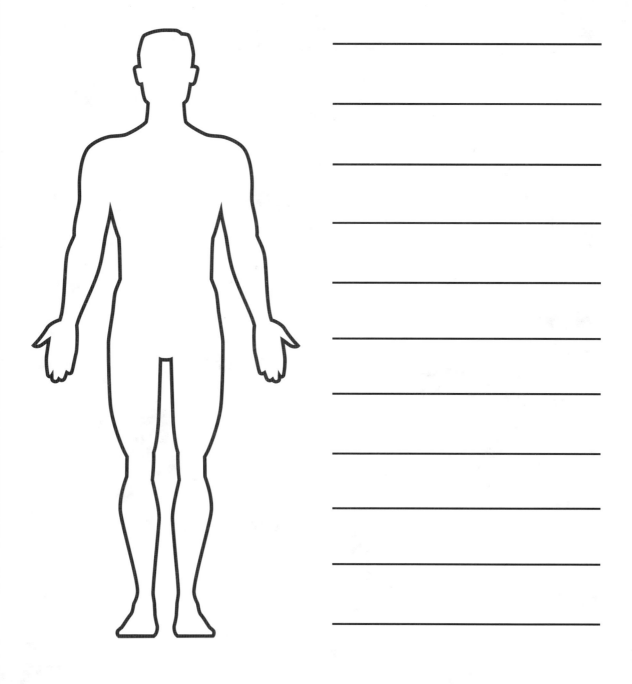

I Feel

"I" statements are a constructive way to communicate your feelings without using blame or negativity. Using the scenarios below, use an "I" statement to effectively communicate how you feel in the situation.

"I" statement: "I feel _____ when you _____. Next time, please _____ ."

Scenario: *Your friend asks others to play at recess but does not include you in the group.*

"I" Statement:

Scenario: *Your parent yells at you to clean your room because it looks awful.*

"I" Statement:

Scenario: *Your sibling borrowed your clothes without asking and then got a stain on them.*

"I" Statement:

Scenario: *You are working on a group project and feel that you are doing more work than your partners.*

"I" Statement:

Watch Your Words

Words can hurt others or make a situation worse. It is important to understand the difference between kind words and angry words. Think back to a situation when you were upset and may have used unkind words, and describe the situation in the top box. List the unkind words you used in the appropriate box. Then list kind words in the box next it. In the redo box, write a kinder approach to solve the problem.

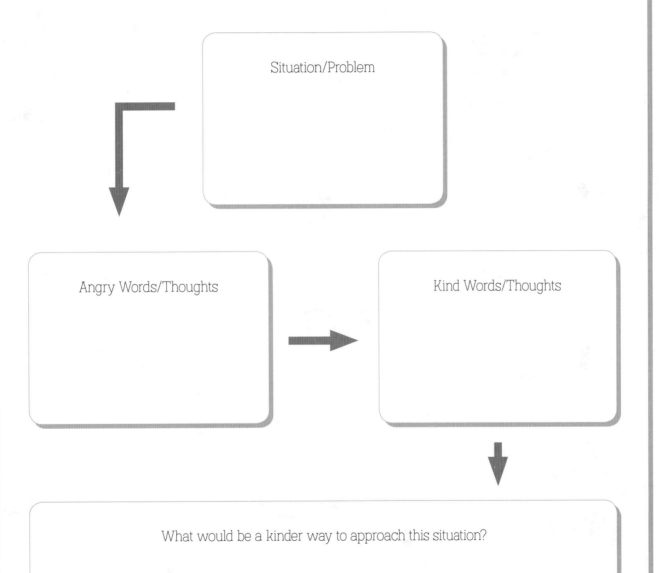

Situation/Problem

Angry Words/Thoughts

Kind Words/Thoughts

What would be a kinder way to approach this situation?

Communicating with Others

Communicating with some people can be easy, while it's harder with others. It is important to communicate positively so that your voice can be heard while you stay in control of your emotions. This activity asks you to identify people in your life with whom you feel comfortable talking with. Identify characteristics that make the person easy to talk to and then strategies you use to communicate with that person. Then think of people who are more difficult to talk to or trigger your feelings. What characteristics make it more difficult to communicate with them? What strategies could help you stay in control when talking to these people?

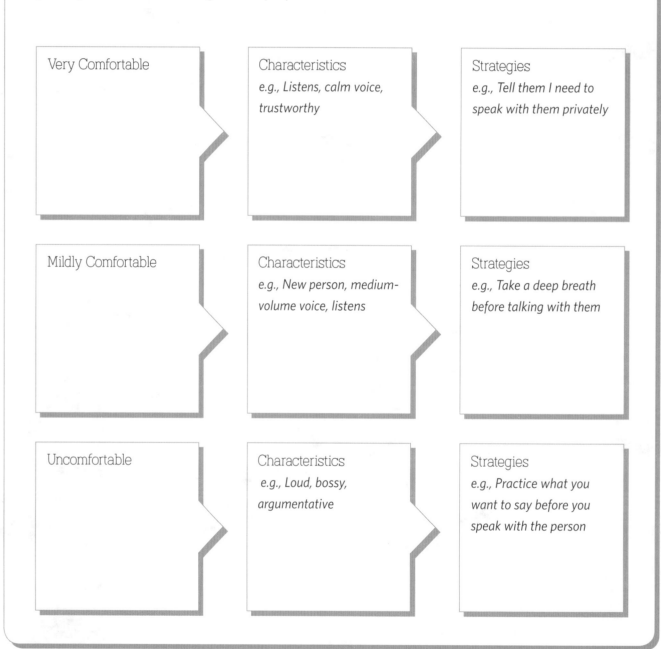

Very Comfortable

Characteristics
e.g., Listens, calm voice, trustworthy

Strategies
e.g., Tell them I need to speak with them privately

Mildly Comfortable

Characteristics
e.g., New person, medium-volume voice, listens

Strategies
e.g., Take a deep breath before talking with them

Uncomfortable

Characteristics
e.g., Loud, bossy, argumentative

Strategies
e.g., Practice what you want to say before you speak with the person

Understanding Family Rules

Every family is unique, with a different set of values and rules. In the boxes below, write down the names of the members of your family who live with you. What are the values in your house? What are the rules? What are the consequences if someone breaks the rules? In the final box, write about rules that seem unfair or difficult for you to follow.

Family Members

Family Values

_____

_____

_____

Family Rules

_____

_____

_____

Consequences

_____

_____

What rules are more difficult for you to follow?
What would you like changed if it were possible?

_____

_____

_____

Friends and Family

Take a minute to think about your relationships with your family members and friends. In the circles below, list family and friends with whom you feel you have a strong positive relationship. In the overlapping area, list common traits about the individuals with whom you feel most comfortable. In the boxes below, list your strengths and weakness in developing relationships.

FAMILY

FRIENDS

My strengths for building relationships:

My weaknesses to work on for building relationships:

Respecting Myself and Others

Define what *respect* means to you, then look up the definition in a dictionary and write it below. What can you do to show respectful behavior through your thoughts, feelings, and actions in the settings listed in the chart? In what situations is it easier to be respectful? In what situations is it more difficult?

What respect means to me:

Definition of respect:

	At Home	At School	In Community
Thoughts			
Emotions/Feelings			
Actions			

Pro-social Behaviors

Practicing pro-social behaviors in calm situations can help you know what to do in other situations, both positive and negative. If you were in the following situations, what would be your actions, thoughts, or feelings? How does your behavior affect your relationship with the other person/people in that situation? What can you learn from these situations that you can apply in the future?

	Actions	Thoughts	Feelings	Affect on Other(s)
Asking for a turn				
Saying something nice to a friend				
Helping a neighbor				
Arguing with a friend or family member				
Make your own:				
Make your own:				

Helpful Behaviors

Begin a discussion with the client on helping behaviors. Challenge the client to become a helper. Ask him or her to identify helping behaviors. Invite the client to complete the worksheet by identifying three different people to help and three different helping behaviors to offer each of these individuals. Discuss with the client his/her expected outcomes for each of these behaviors and make note of them in the appropriate space. Decide on a deadline for completing these behaviors. Invite the client to take this worksheet home for reference.

#1

Person:

Helping Behavior:

Expected Outcome:

#2

Person:

Helping Behavior:

Expected Outcome:

#3

Person:

Helping Behavior:

Expected Outcome:

Helpful Self

In the space below, create a collage of words, writing, and images describing how you can help others. Think about how you can help others at home, school, or in the community. How does being helpful make you feel? How do you think others view you when you are being helpful?

Behavioral Sequencing

The next three activities are designed to be used together as one exercise. The following pages will focus on helping the client recognize moments in time where they may have lost control of their actions, thoughts or feelings. The client will work on sequencing behaviors, recognizing triggers and positive problem reframing. Activities can be completed in one session or over multiple sessions depending on preference.

Behavioral Sequencing: Part 1

Think of a situation when you lost control of your emotions or behavior. In the boxes below depict that situation from beginning to end, like a comic strip style story. Use pictures or words to describe your feelings and actions before, during and after the situation.

Example:

Problem	Before	During	After
Suspended for disruptive behavior in the classroom.	Joe said something that was not true.	Got upset. My face got red and my heart was beating fast. Began to argue with Joe.	Teacher asked me to leave classroom and talk with principal. Started arguing with teacher.

Problem	Before	During	After

Tipping Point: Part 2

Complete the Behavior Sequencing activity prior to completing this activity. Identify the moment when you lost control of your actions, thoughts or feelings. Depict how that feels in the diagram below. Next list ways that help you stay in control.

	Thoughts	Feelings	Actions
Tipping Point	*I could not stop thinking about what occurred.*	*I was so angry and my body got hot.*	*I started yelling.*
Strategies to Stay in Control	*Think of a calming place.*	*Deep breathing.*	*Count to 10 before acting.*

Behavioral Sequencing Redo: Part 3

Review your original problem and your strategies to stay in control. Rewrite your problem with your strategies in mind. How can you change your actions to resolve your problem with a more positive outcome?

Problem	Before	During	After

Control Cards

Control cards are visual cues to help keep you in control and reduce negative thinking when faced with a challenging situation. Following is an example of simple rules to follow when you get angry. Complete your own personal cards to help keep you in control.

Example:

Control of My Anger
What I am going to do: *Take a deep breath.*
Positive thought: *I am in control of my actions.*
Rules: *I will keep my hands to myself. I will only use kind words or none at all.*

Control of My Anger
What I am going to do:
Positive thought:
Rules:

Control of My Frustration
What I am going to do:
Positive thought:
Rules:

Reframing Thoughts

One way to recognize patterns of negative thinking is to practice reframing your thoughts in a low-stress environment. In the scenarios below, identify unhelpful or negative thoughts that you might experience and then replace them with positive thoughts.

1. *Situation:* You missed the bus to school.

Unhelpful Thoughts:

_____

Helpful Thoughts:

_____

2. *Situation:* You are told you cannot do something.

Unhelpful Thoughts:

_____

Helpful Thoughts:

_____

3. *Situation:* Your plans are canceled.

Unhelpful Thoughts:

_____

Helpful Thoughts:

_____

4. *Situation:* A friend hurts your feelings.

Unhelpful Thoughts:

_____

Helpful Thoughts:

_____

Change of Mind

Read each statement and provide alternative, empowering thoughts.

All-or-Nothing Statements	Positive Reframing
I will never get this work done.	*I will finish. I will complete this task one step at a time.*
No one cares about my opinion.	
This is too difficult.	
It's not going to work.	
This is the best I can do.	
I am not good at this.	
This is easy for everyone but me.	
I can't do anything right.	

Building Emotional Vocabulary

Are you ever at a loss for words when you become upset? Is it difficult to explain to others how you are feeling? This activity is designed to build your emotional database and help you recognize a variety of emotions. For each emotion, write three other emotions that have similar meaning.

Happy	Calm	Frustrated

Mad	Sad	Scared

Linking Emotions, Thoughts, and Feelings

People feel different emotions in different situations. What makes you happy or angry may not be the same for others. For the emotions listed below, complete the sentences based on how you feel.

Happy

I am happy when _____.

When I am happy, my thoughts are _____.

When I am happy, my body feels _____.

Angry

I get angry when _____.

When I am angry, my thoughts are _____.

When I am angry, my body feels _____.

Sad

I am sad when _____.

When I am sad, my thoughts are _____.

When I am sad, my body feels _____.

Calm

I am calm when _____.

When I am calm, my thoughts are _____.

When I am calm, my body feels _____.

Frustrated

I get frustrated when _____.

When I am frustrated, my thoughts are _____.

When I am frustrated, my body feels _____.

Feeling States

PART 1

Have the client name as many feelings as they know and write each of them on a separate piece of paper. Help the client build their feeling vocabulary if needed. Have them pull the pieces of paper one by one out of a bowl and use body language and facial expressions to relay the feeling message. If possible, use a mirror so the client can see their own expressions.

PART 2

Get a new piece of paper for each of the feeling states from Part 1. Write the name of the feeling at the top of each paper. Have the client draw or cut and paste magazine images to depict each of these feeling states and write a sentence about why a person might feel this way.

PART 3

Each week, pick one or two of the feeling states identified in Part 1 and review them. Instruct the client to spend the remainder of the week paying attention in their daily life to identify someone who is experiencing this feeling state. Challenge the client to find a way to help or to be with someone while they are experiencing this feeling. Examples: If you notice someone is happy, find a way to experience this joy with them. If you see someone is sad, offer a listening ear or an encouraging statement.

PART 4

In the next session, pull out one of the papers with a feeling state explored in Part 3. On the back, have the client journal or draw what it was like to identify that feeling state in another person and what it was like to help them.

How large is the client's feeling vocabulary? Did the client need help planning ideas for how to identify and help a person in each feeling state? Has the client's view of self changed now that they are able to be more empathic toward others' feelings?

 # Peace Chain

Write down peaceful, calming words on the paper strips below. Cut them out and connect the pieces to form a chain with staples or tape. Use the chain as a visual reminder of calming words and how strong they can be when linked together.

Peaceful Actions

What does it mean to be peaceful? Write or illustrate what peace looks like in the box below. How can you show peace at home, at school, and in the community?

Peaceful Behavior at Home	Peaceful Behavior at School	Peaceful Behavior in the Community

Thinking Peace

When I feel angry, my thoughts look like this:

When I feel peaceful, my thoughts look like this:

How can I create more peace in my life and the lives of others?

Recipe for Success

Anger has different triggers, feelings, and responses. Different approaches work for different individuals. What recipe works for you? Identify your triggers, your anger responses, people who can support you, and strategies to help you keep your cool.

Recipe for Success

I get angry when _____

_____.

My body feels like _____

_____.

My usual response is _____

_____.

I can control by actions by talking to _____

_____.

I will use these strategies to stay calm: _____

_____.

It takes me _____ (amount of time) to calm myself.

Yell It from the Mountaintop

Write down a recurring thought that is creating feelings of anger. Write it large and in bold as if you were yelling it from a mountaintop. When you are finished, take the paper, crumble it up, and then throw it in the trash, releasing the negative thought. Note how your body felt while writing the thought and how it felt after releasing it.

10-Point Check-In

This page is a quick "cheat sheet" on grounding and coping skills. Start at the top and work your way to the bottom. At the end, discuss with your therapist or journal about how you felt prior to starting this exercise and how you felt when you completed this exercise.

10	Take 10 deep breaths
9	Name 9 things you see
8	Name 8 people who support you
7	Name 7 colors
6	Name 6 things that make you happy
5	Take 5 deep breaths
4	Name 4 things you hear
3	Name 3 things that you can touch
2	Take 2 deep breaths
1	How do you feel now?

Letter of Thanks

Expressing gratitude can have a positive impact on your mental and physical health. Write a letter to a person for whom you are thankful. Tell them why they are special and how they help you.

Dear ,_____

Thank you for _____

_____

_____

_____

_____

_____

_____

_____

_____

_____

_____

_____

_____

Sincerely,

_____

Little Victories

Time to recognize your accomplishments. Creating change is not easy, and it is important to evaluate your efforts in order to build confidence in your abilities. Write your goal for the week and for the future. For each day, note your accomplishments, big (e.g., aced a test) and small (e.g., woke up on time, took a walk instead of hitting the wall).

Weekly Goal:

Long-Term Goal:

	Daily Accomplishments
Sunday	
Monday	
Tuesday	
Wednesday	
Thursday	
Friday	
Saturday	

Major Accomplishments:

Room for Improvement:

Grateful Feelings

There are times when it is difficult to see the good in our lives. We are quick to feel anger and unable to see the positive people and things going on around us. Take a minute to write something in each shape for which you are grateful and color in the shape. This can be a reminder of the positive things in your life.

Anxiety

A nxiety is a necessary bodily response, alerting the body to potential danger and enabling the "fight or flight" response. Physiological responses are the body's way of trying to be proactive to react to what is going on in the environment. Anxiety becomes an issue when the physiological responses are triggered more often and reinforced by negative thinking and worry. Worry takes over, and small issues cause overwhelming feelings and general lack of control.

To reduce the impact of anxiety and identify coping strategies, individuals must understand how anxiety is triggered, how it manifests, and how it is impairing daily functions. Anxiety can also present as a comorbid symptom along with other diagnoses, such as depression, trauma, and/or attention deficit hyperactivity disorder. Because children and adolescents may experience periods of increased anxiety, teaching them coping skills can help reduce symptoms and allow the client to move on.

Getting to Know Your Worry

1. Describe a recent situation when you experienced some anxiety. Remember to describe the what, where, and why of this situation. _____

   _____

   _____

2. Was there anything you could have changed about this situation to make it less anxiety provoking? Was there anything you could have changed to make it more peaceful? _____

   _____

   _____

   _____

3. List the things you were not able to change about this situation. What didn't you have control over?

   _____

   _____

   _____

4. Describe a recent situation where you felt peaceful or at ease. _____

   _____

   _____

5. Describe your thoughts regarding the peaceful situation. What were you thinking? What were you feeling? _____

   _____

   _____

6. When in an anxiety-provoking situation, what would change for you if you could accept your thoughts and the situation for what they are? _____

   _____

   _____

Anxiety Hierarchy

Developing a hierarchy of fears or anxiety is a helpful way for you and the client to prioritize what is impacting them most. It's recommended to develop the hierarchy together in-session. Work together to identify situations that trigger anxiety, but also how the client's body feels and reacts at each stage. Level 1 should be something that causes little to no anxiety. Level 5 should be something that causes the client the most anxiety.

Start by providing situations that might be stressful if the client is not able to do so. Keep the Anxiety Hierarchy chart handy and refer to it during other exercises. As therapy progresses repeat this process to identify emerging sources of anxiety. In subsequent sessions, the client can begin filling it in themselves with fewer prompts.

Anxiety Hierarchy

Our bodies respond and react to worry in different ways and with varying intensities. It is important to understand what situations create worry and how the body responds. Below is a pyramid that will represent your response to anxiety or worries. In the largest block (1) list everyday activities that cause little to no stress. Continue listing examples of situations that increase intensity through blocks 2-4. In the smallest block (5), list activities that cause or would cause the greatest amount of worry.

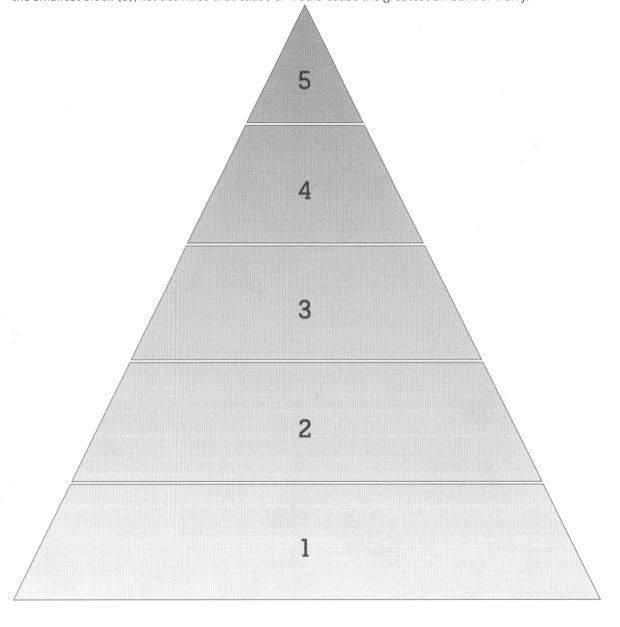

Your Worry

Everyone's worry looks different. In the circle below, draw what you believe your worry looks like. Name your worry. This will help you externalize your worry, so that it is not something inside of you, but something tangible that you can start to confront and make "go away."

"Good" Worry vs. "Bad" Worry

This activity is designed to help you understand and separate good worry verses bad worry. For instance, "good" worry might be worrying about an upcoming test, which motivates you to study. "Bad" worry might be the worry that prevents you from completing your day-to-day routine (such as, not going to school because you are so worried about the grade you will get on a test). Write down several of your examples of good and bad worry.

Good Worry	Bad Worry

Detective

Discuss with client how anxious feelings are often based on irrational thoughts. Have the client identify one anxious thought. Ask them to pretend to become a detective and find as many facts and clues as possible to dispute this anxious thought. Have the client replace their anxious thought with a healthier and more realistic self-statement. Repeat the exercise as many times as needed for each additional worrying thought.

Anxious feeling comes from this thought:

Clues that disprove your anxious thought:

Rate how often the client is experiencing this anxious thinking. Have the client review this exercise each time the thought recurs. Measure any changes in frequency and intensity.

Realistic thought/self-statement:

Weighing Your Worries

With every new situation, there are benefits (pros) and worries (cons) that can influence your actions. Write down an event or thought that is causing you to worry. Let's weigh out the pros and cons and determine an action(s) you can take to resolve what is worrying you. For instance, say you are concerned about joining a new soccer team. Pros could be: make new friends and improve skills. Cons could be: no one will like me, feeling like you are not good enough. At the bottom of the page, write your action plan including coping skills and reframing of thoughts to help you overcome your worry. For instance, I will practice my soccer skills before the first practice in order to feel more confident and prepared about joining the new team.

PROS

CONS

Problem & Actions I Could Take

_____

_____

_____

Responses, Reactions, and Feelings

On the outline below draw, color, or write what happens to your body or within your body when you get worried, anxious, and/or nervous. Write down how these various body reactions make you feel and what they make you think. Think about what this means for you and how you can problem solve around these various body reactions, responses, and feelings.

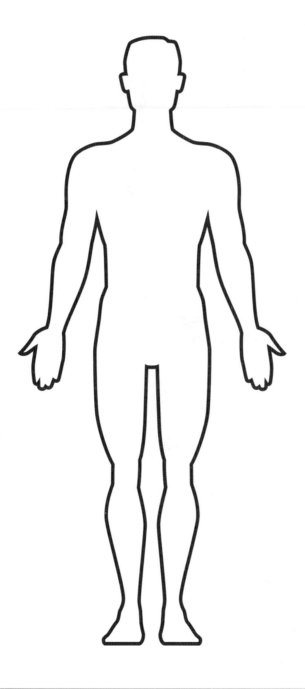

How Do You
Respond to Your Worry?

We all respond to worry differently. There are mental and physical responses. (Examples of each are listed below.) In this activity, identify an event that causes minimal anxiety and one that causes high levels of anxiety. Are there differences? Are there similarities? Are there different coping skills you can use, based on how you respond?

Examples:

Mental	*Difficulty concentrating, troubling thoughts, imagining worst-case scenario*
Physical	*Restlessness, racing heart, stomachache, shaking or trembling, sleeplessness, dizziness, muscle tension, clammy hands*

	Low-Stress/Low-Anxiety Event	High-Stress/High-Anxiety Event
Mental		
Physical		
Coping Strategies		

Thoughts and Feelings Log

Journaling is a helpful way to gain insight on the impact of negative thoughts or worries. To better understand the impact of your anxiety, journal about your intrusive thoughts. When a negative thought or recurring thought happens, write down the event, your feelings, how long the feelings lasted, and what happened as a result of the worry. (Did you miss out on an opportunity? Were you able to rejoin a group? Did you avoid an activity or person?)

Event (Time of Day, People Involved, Situation)	Negative Thought or Worry	Feelings & Why	How Long the Feelings Lasted	Outcome

Talking with Others

Think about the different groups of people with whom you interact on a daily basis. List specific individuals within each group, when possible (e.g., Family – mom, dad, sister, aunt, etc.). What is your level of comfort with each member? Levels of comfort can be different within each level. Describe comfort level on a scale from 1-5, with 1 being very easy to 5 being more difficult.

	Comfort Level	What I Feel Comfortable Saying or Doing
Family members		
Friends		
Community members (e.g., teacher, minister, coach)		
Authority figures (e.g., police officer, doctor)		
Strangers		

Helpful Thinking

In the scenarios that follow, identify an unhelpful thought or negative thought that might be initially experienced; replace it with a positive thought.

1. You are asked to speak in front of a large group.

   Unhelpful thought: _____

   Positive thought: _____

2. You need to complete a large project in a short amount of time.

   Unhelpful thought: _____

   Positive thought: _____

3. The teacher gives you a pop quiz.

   Unhelpful thought: _____

   Positive thought: _____

4. You are starting at a new school and do not know anyone.

   Unhelpful thought: _____

   Positive thought: _____

5. You are sitting next to someone who is sick.

   Unhelpful thought: _____

   Positive thought: _____

Trust Bubble

Think about the people in your life who are supportive and trustworthy (existing friends, family). What do you look for in a friend? In the circles below, identify positive characteristics of yourself and of friends and adults whom you trust. What do you have in common? What makes them unique? What helps you to trust them? Write or draw your responses below. Highlight common characteristics that all three groups share.

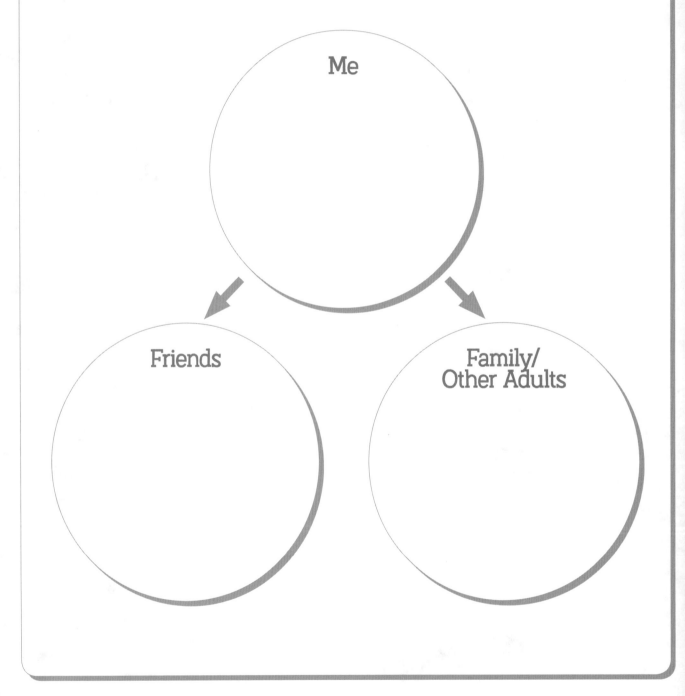

Assertiveness Regulator

Think about the differences among passive, assertive, and aggressive behaviors. For each area, describe what nonverbal cues look like (eye contact, posture, rate of speech, movement of arms/hand).
Then, describe situations or people that are more likely to make you behave passively, assertively, or aggressively. For example, you may feel more passive in a large group but more assertive in a one-on-one setting. You may be more aggressive with siblings and more passive with authority figures.

1. Passive

Nonverbal cues: _____

Individuals: _____

Settings: _____

2. Assertive

Nonverbal cues: _____

Individuals: _____

Settings: _____

3. Aggressive

Nonverbal cues: _____

Individuals: _____

Settings: _____

Three Wishes

Imagine yourself in a social setting. Write three wishes you would like to be granted to help make the situation easier. Then, rewrite each wish using a personal strength or coping skill you could use to make your wish a reality.

I wish I were more _____

_____.

I can be more _____ by _____

_____.

I wish I were more _____

_____.

I can be more _____ by _____

_____.

I wish I were more _____

_____.

I can be more _____ by _____

_____.

To Do, Won't Do List

Anxiety can occur when we take on too much, saying "yes" to everything asked of us. To be more assertive, we must prioritize what needs to get done and what can wait. Below, write down a list of things you have to do and other responsibilities that are causing you stress. From that list, identify what needs to be done immediately, things you want to or need to do but not right away, and other things that you do not have time to or do not want to do.

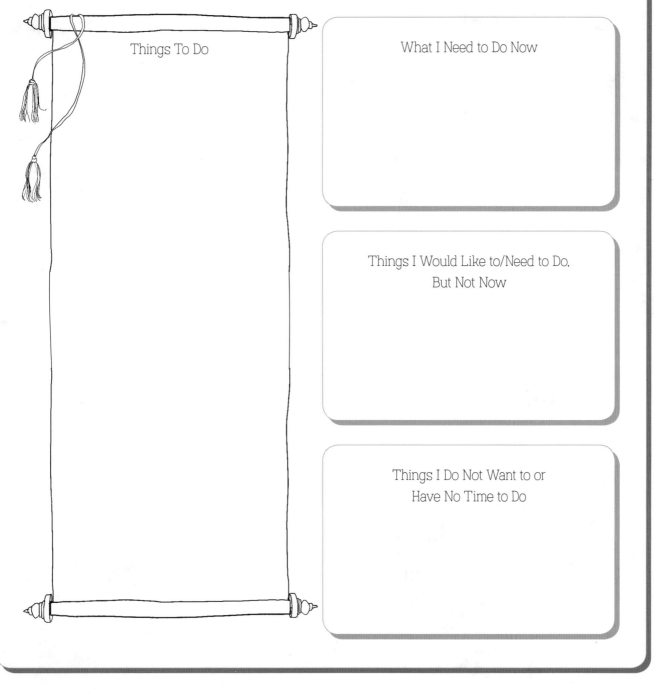

Things To Do

What I Need to Do Now

Things I Would Like to/Need to Do, But Not Now

Things I Do Not Want to or Have No Time to Do

Pro-social Behaviors

Conquering anxiety in social situations can be done by building confidence in our abilities and by practicing pro-social behaviors. Think about the situations listed in the chart and remember a time you were in that situation or imagine that it happened. Describe your actions, thoughts, and feelings. How did your behaviors affect other people involved in that situation? What can you learn from your experiences to help you face upcoming challenges at home, at school, or in the community?

	Actions	Thoughts	Feelings	Affect on Other(s)
Introducing yourself to a classmate				
Talking with a teacher				
Working with a group of classmates				
Asking others to play				
Make your own:				

When were you the most confident? _____

When were you the least confident? _____

What negative thoughts do you need to reframe? _____

Stressed Out!

We are faced with stressful situations each day. To cope, we need to recognize what we should do (use coping skills) and what we shouldn't do (engage in negative thinking). Fill in the worksheet using an example of a recent situation that stressed you out and things you can do to cope versus things that probably won't help.

Stressful situation: _____

_____

Procrastinate	Talk to a friend	Cry	Yell
Avoid the situation	Breathe	Ask for help	
Take a break	Use positive self-talk	Shut down	

I can ...	I shouldn't ...

What helps you most in dealing with stress, frustration, fear, or anxiety?

Fear/Anxiety Self-Statements

In the box below, write about or draw a social situation that gives you fear/anxiety (for example, my fear is being teased by classmates). Then, in the lightning bolt, label this fear and turn it into a statement or belief about yourself (I worry that this would mean that no one likes me). Finally, in the sun, write the ways this self-statement is not rational. List evidence/facts about yourself to combat this fear (I have friends, so it's not true that no one likes me.)

How rational is your fear? How likely is it to happen? _____

How rational is your self-statement connected to this fear? _____

What evidence do you have about yourself that proves that this self-statement is not true?

_____

Red Light, Yellow Light, Green Light

This activity is designed to help you identify a worry, problem-solve for the worry, and make a good decision regarding your worry. Use the traffic light below to remind you to stop and identify the worry (red), come up with a plan (yellow), and act (green). As learned in previous activities, some worry is good, and some is bad. Use this activity to help you decide if the worry you are experiencing is "bad" worry that can be addressed in a positive way.

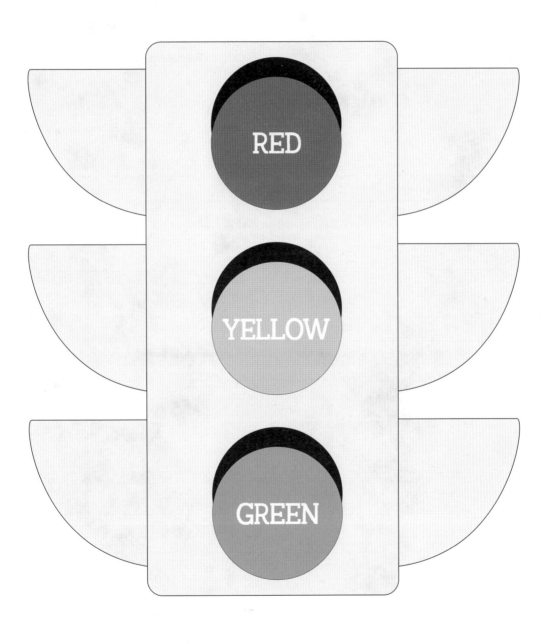

Creating Your Own Coping Kit

No matter what difficult emotion or thought a client is having, it is helpful for them to have a kit ready to address it. Assist your client in problem solving to create their own kit at home. It's great if you are able to have various items in your office that could be used in a kit, but if not, you can help your client identify what items could be helpful. The items chosen should help the client think positively and relax (perhaps a stuffed animal, a photo of a loved one, a puzzle or game, a card with positive messages written on it).

On the suitcases below, have the client write or draw items that they could keep in a box, bag, or suitcase to have ready to help them cope with difficult emotions or thoughts.

Stay Calm Checklist

When presented with anxiety, one can feel out of control. Sometimes, we rely on tactics that are unhealthy, such as avoidance, insisting on routine, or predicting the worst outcome, instead of trying something new. Although these strategies may provide temporary relief, they do not help in the long run. Together with your therapist or parent, create a list of strategies that are helpful in reducing your level of anxiety. Write down your strategies on the following clipboard to highlight what you can do to stay calm.

CHECKLIST

✔

✔

✔

✔

✔

✔

✔

Circle of Control

Many of us, when anxious, will try to find things we can control. This is due to feeling out of control or overwhelmed. This activity is designed to help you identify what you have control over versus what you do not have control over. Think of your most anxiety-provoking situations, and use the circles to identify what you have control over and what is not in your control. Process this further with your therapist for ways to focus more on what you can actually control. This will help lessen your anxiety and overwhelming feelings.

Things Out of
My Control

Things I
Can Control

Managing Expectations of Control

This activity is designed to help you identify what level of control you have in various situations. Next to each situation, mark the box that accurately depicts how much control you have.

	No Control	Some Control	Total Control
1. If you will have fun at your family event			
2. If you will get along with your family			
3. If someone likes you at school			
4. If you are a nice person			
5. If your friend listens to your advice			
6. If you will do well on an upcoming test			
7. If your friends like your shoes			
8. If you will break the school's basketball record			
9. If you will make all your catches and passes in your game			
10. If you listen and follow directions			
11. If your grandmother passes away			
12. If it will rain during your upcoming vacation			
13. If the teacher will grade you fairly			
14. If your girlfriend/boyfriend breaks up with you			
15. If you wake up in time for school			
16. If you achieve your goals			

Controlling Your Thoughts

Do you ever wish you could control the "volume" of your thoughts or slow down racing thoughts? Is there so much noise in your mind that it is hard to concentrate? This activity is designed to assist you in identifying your anxious thoughts and worries and identifying coping skills to "turn down" the volume of your reaction to these thoughts. In the "loud volume" area, write something that is bothering you and making your thoughts/worries feel loud, as well as the thoughts you are having. Then identify what coping skills could turn down the volume of your reaction to a medium level and write them in the "medium volume" area; in the "low volume" area, write what could help turn the volume down to low.

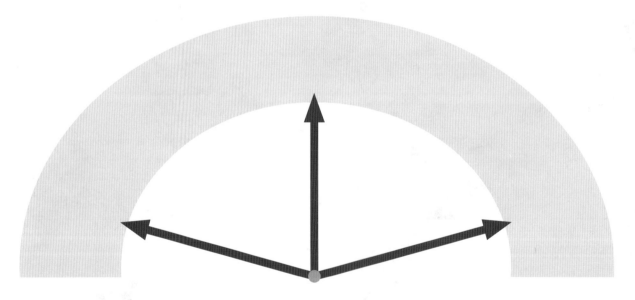

What could bring my thoughts
down to medium volume?

What could bring my thoughts
down to low volume?

What are my "loud-volume"
thoughts/worries?
What caused them?

What Will Work?

This activity is designed to assist in identifying helpful coping skills for managing anxiety. In the first balloon, write or draw the coping skills you have found helpful for managing your anxiety. In the next balloon, write or draw the coping skills you have found to be less effective.

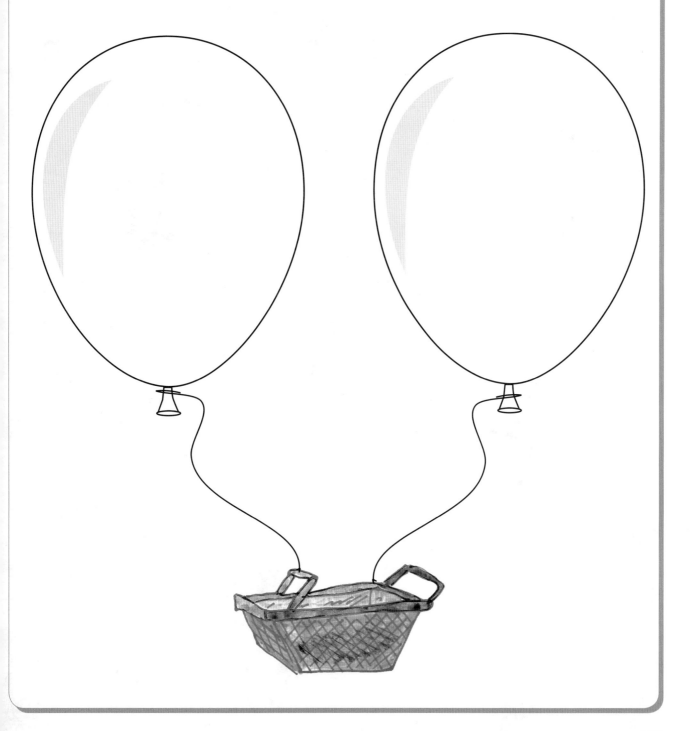

How Do We Get There?

This activity is designed to help you get from point A to point B, start to finish. Start moving through the maze, and in the dead ends, identify and write or draw difficulties, bad thoughts/worries, and what could prevent you from getting to the finish line. On the path that leads to the finish line, write or draw things that will help, or did help, you overcome the worry/anxiety.

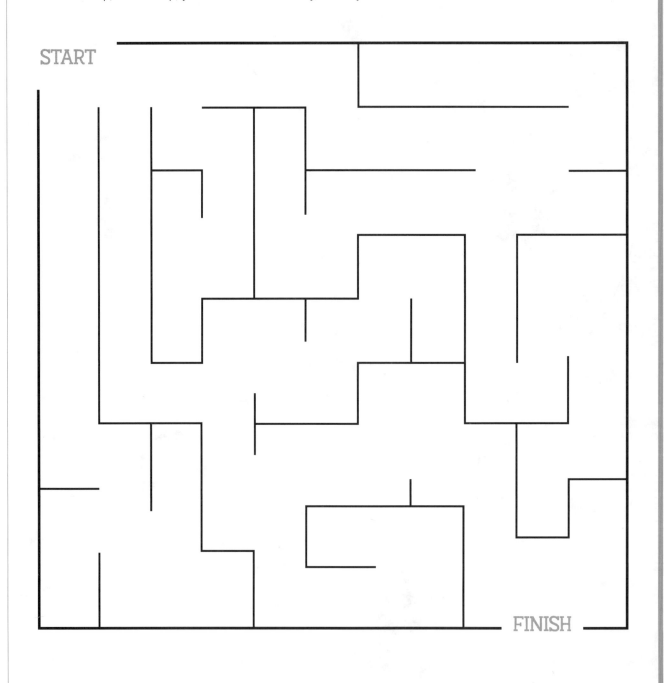

Stop, Rewind, Rethink

Begin discussions on how a client's anxious feelings can impact their thoughts. Provide some examples as a warm-up. Assist the client in identifying how these anxious feelings are not based in realistic thinking.

After this warm-up time, review the exercise instructions with the client on the following page. Observe if the client can complete the worksheet on his/her own and offer assistance as needed.

Once the worksheet is completed, review on his/her observations related to anxious thinking. Empower their ability to take control over these thoughts and train their brain to "rethink" these thoughts to be more reality based.

Consider making copies of this blank worksheet to send home, and encourage use each time an anxious thought appears. Revisit these completed worksheets at next session to measure usage and effectiveness.

Stop, Rewind, Rethink

Identify an anxiety-provoking thought and list this thought in the first box. Observe how this anxious thought is not based in reality, and in the second box, note how this thought is skipping rational thinking. Make note of how to disprove this anxious thought. In the third box, make note of a positive and healthy self-talk phrase to combat the anxious thought. This might include facts to disprove your anxious thought.

STOP ⏹

Identify your anxious thought. Think of a self-talk phrase to stop this thought and write it in the box.

REWIND ⏪

Notice that your brain is skipping over rational thinking and going into worry thinking. Write down how you will calm your brain and rewind back into rational thinking.

RETHINK ☁

Identify facts to disprove your anxious thinking and write them in the box.

Within Reach!

Declare your goals! What goal are you trying to reach? Indicate what feelings, thoughts, and actions you want to increase and decrease. To help you be more prepared, indicate any challenges you may find along the way, what coping methods you could use, and who could support you on your journey to reach your goals.

Goal:	
Feelings/Thoughts/Actions to Increase:	Feelings/Thoughts/Actions to Decrease:
Possible Challenges:	Coping Skills:
Support Team:	

Goal:	
Feelings/Thoughts/Actions to Increase:	Feelings/Thoughts/Actions to Decrease:
Possible Challenges:	Coping Skills:
Support Team:	

26 Positive Traits

When faced with worries and fears, it is often difficult to recognize your personal strengths. List 26 things that describe what makes you unique and great!

1.		14.	
2.		15.	
3.		16.	
4.		17.	
5.		18.	
6.		19.	
7.		20.	
8.		21.	
9.		22.	
10.		23.	
11.		24.	
12.		25.	
13.		26.	

Self-Care Routine

Become more mindful of taking time each day to nourish your mind and body. Having a self-care routine allows you to focus, release, or reset each day. Keep track of your self-care activities for one week. Be mindful of taking time for yourself to strengthen your mind (such as reading, mediation, journaling) and body (walking, dancing, yoga for example).

Sun.
Mind: _____
Body: _____

Mon.
Mind: _____
Body: _____

Tue.
Mind: _____
Body: _____

Wed.
Mind: _____
Body: _____

Thurs.
Mind: _____
Body: _____

Fri.
Mind: _____
Body: _____

Sat.
Mind: _____
Body: _____

Staying in the Present

Discuss why staying in the present moment is so important.

• What keeps us out of the present moment and thinking about the future or the past?

Focus on thoughts and feelings that keep us in the present and contrast those that keep us out of the present.

• What body sensations do you notice?

• Why is staying in the present difficult?

• Where does your mind tend to wonder when trying to stay present moment?

Staying in the Present

When we worry, we tend to feel anxious about the future or what has happened in the past—it is difficult for us to stay in the present. This activity is designed to assist you in finding ways to stay in the present moment. Think about what you might need to stay in the present moment, and on and around the box, write the sayings or reminders and draw the items that can help you.

Let's Box It Away

The boxes below serve as a metaphor for removing the worry and anxiety from your mind. Write or draw "things" that make you worry, fearful, or anxious in or around the box. Fold the paper, as you would fold the top of boxes, to represent putting your anxiety away. Discuss your feelings and thoughts related to this activity.

You're Not Alone

Although anxiety may produce feelings of isolation and distress, you can manage your symptoms and feel success. Research four different famous individuals who also struggle(d) with anxiety. What have they achieved in their life? What helped these individuals to be successful?

Name:

Information:

Name:

Information:

Name:

Information:

Name:

Information:

Relaxation Rolls

This is a game to help you practice muscle relaxation. Roll a single die and perform the relaxation technique next to the number you roll. You can also list your own calming strategies for Round 2 and practice each when you roll the die.

Round 1

1. Clench your toes, count to three, then relax your toes.

2. Close your eyes tightly, count to three, then relax your eyes and face.

3. Clench your teeth, count to three, then relax your jaw.

4. Tighten your fists, count to three, then relax your hands.

5. Tighten your calf muscles, count to three, then relax your legs.

6. Tighten your stomach, count to three, then relax your stomach.

Round 2

1.

2.

3.

4.

5.

6.

Mandala

Coloring or drawing a mandala, a geometric pattern that represents the universe, is a good exercise to address anxiety and build control. This gives you something to focus on and design just how you want it designed. Color the following mandala and allow yourself to focus and relax.

Anxiety the Alien

In the following activity, assist the client in identifying what might grow or shrink the feelings of anxiety. Once the exercise is completed, you can revisit this metaphor as many times as needed to encourage the client to use the "shrinking potion" throughout the week when the anxiety grows. You might encourage the client to take home the completed exercise page as a reminder of the "shrinking potions" he/she has developed to prompt use of these healthy thoughts and behaviors daily.

- Did the client understand the concept that thoughts and behaviors can feed anxiety and make it bigger?
- Discuss what happens inside the client's body when anxiety is at its biggest vs. at its smallest.
- Encourage the client to use the "shrinking potion" throughout the week when the anxiety grows.

Anxiety the Alien

Imagine your feelings of anxiety taking on the form of an alien being. In the middle, draw what this "anxiety alien" looks like. Think about what thoughts and behaviors "feed" this anxiety alien to make it bigger and write these on the crackers to the left. Think about the thoughts and behaviors that help to "shrink" the anxiety alien and write those on the bottles of "shrinking potion" on the right.

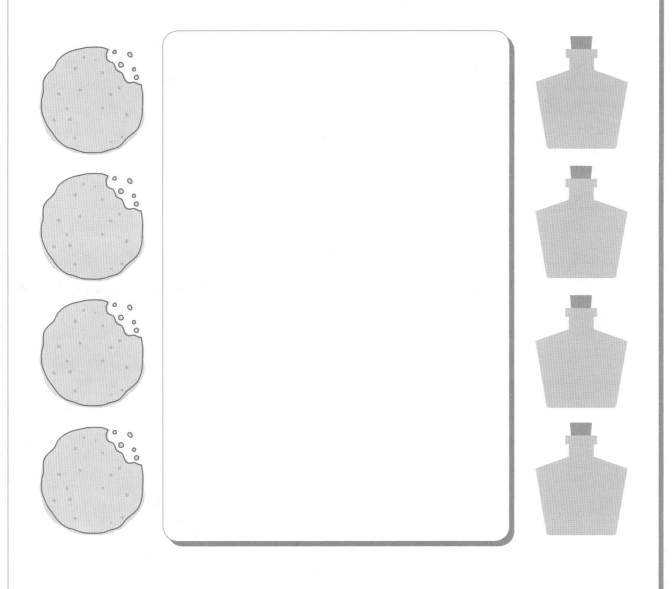

SECTION

Depression

Sadness can be described in many ways, such as feeling gloomy, hopeless, or down and out. Everyone has felt some level of sadness, whether it was temporary or longer lasting. Sadness is a healthy emotion if you are able to use coping skills to help it fade. Unfortunately, many people experience isolation, crippling sadness, and withdrawal from normal activities, all elements of clinical depression. A variety of individual factors, such as biological and environmental components, can also influence the onset of depression.

This section focuses on unique approaches to addressing negative thoughts, feelings, and behaviors related to depression in children and adolescents. Activities building cognitive skills encourage clients to become more aware of their mood, behavioral patterns and triggers, and better understand the expression of their emotions. Relationship-coaching activities help clients build confidence, self-esteem, and create a supportive alliance. Competency-building activities focus on realistic thinking, coping skills, and positive problem solving. Lastly, brain-based learning activities encourage clients to reflect on motivation, increase positive feelings, develop a care plan, and establish healthy habits.

Understanding Your Mood

1. What does having a low mood look like? Describe how your body feels and what your behavior looks like._____

_____

_____

2. What does having a positive mood look like? Describe how your body feels and what your behavior looks like._____

_____

_____

3. Describe a recent situation when you experienced low mood. Remember to describe the what, where, and why of this situation. _____

_____

_____

4. Was there anything you could have changed about this situation to make it less upsetting? Was there anything you could have changed to make it more bearable? _____

_____

_____

_____

5. Describe a recent situation when you were in a great mood. Who was present? What were you doing?_____

_____

_____

6. What kind of activities can you do to help increase positive mood?_____

_____

_____

_____

Mood Tracking

When you are upset or depressed, it can seem like you always feel that way. Use this chart to track your feelings for the week. Give yourself an overall rating for the day. Then, note times during the day when you experienced highs and lows. Note the time of the day, activities you were doing, and how your body felt. At the end of the week, review your chart and highlight any trends or triggers you may have noticed. What strategies can you use to prevent or overcome periods of low mood?

	Overall Daily Mood Rating (1–10, with 1 being awful and 10 being great)	Elevated Mood (list activities going on, time of day, how your body felt)	Low Mood (list activities going on, time of day, how your body felt)
Monday			
Tuesday			
Wednesday			
Thursday			
Friday			
Saturday			
Sunday			

Building Your Defense

Building Your Defense is a resource to allow clients to define individual triggers to depression and brainstorm positive ways to protect or mitigate their feelings of sadness. Discuss any factors that triggered the depressed feelings. Explore how to prevent escalation and negative self-talk. Consider using some of these follow-up questions to direct and enhance conversation during the activity.

- What would this shield be made of?

- What protective qualities would it possess?

- Where would the client like to carry or use this shield?

- What is it like after the shield has been used?

- How does the client feel after using the shield?

Building Your Defenses

In the "Trigger" box, draw or write about an event or thought that causes you to have depressed feelings. Next, imagine if you could insert a shield to protect yourself from experiencing these feelings, and draw or write these protective elements on the shield. In the last box, draw or write what would happen next.

TRIGGER

SHIELD

OUTCOME

Social Interaction and Mood

Does your mood impact your social interactions with others? Do you find yourself reaching out to others or isolating yourself? For the next week, track your mood and rate your level of social interaction. What strategies can you use to help increase positive interactions with others?

	Describe Mood	Notable Events	Social Interaction
Example	*Tired, irritable*	*Large assignment due & difficulty getting started*	*Stayed to myself, ate dinner with my parents, didn't speak much*
Monday			
Tuesday			
Wednesday			
Thursday			
Friday			
Saturday			
Sunday			

People Around Me

This activity is designed to help reduce feelings of isolation by encouraging you to recognize helpful people in your life. In the circle below, list people who know and support you. Include family, friends, community members, teachers, coaches. Then, answer the questions that follow.

My Support Network

Who am I comfortable talking to when I feel lonely?

In my family: _____

At school: _____

In the community: _____

Who do I feel comfortable asking for help?

In my family: _____

At school: _____

In the community: _____

Support Chain

Create a support chain as a visual reminder that you are not alone. On the paper strips below, write the names of people in your life to whom you can talk when you have a problem. Remember to include family, friends, coaches, teachers, neighbors, etc. Cut them out and connect the pieces to form a chain with staples or tape. Use the chain as a visual reminder of how strong your support chain is.

My Feelings

Complete the sentences below with the first thing that comes to mind. If it is difficult to think of something, make a note and discuss maybe why this is with your therapist.

I feel happy when _____

I feel sad when _____

I feel confused when _____

I feel scared when _____

I feel angry when _____

I feel proud when _____

I feel loved when _____

I feel jealous when _____

I feel excited when _____

I feel accepted when _____

I feel silly when _____

I feel sorry when _____

I feel strong when _____

I feel embarrassed when _____

I feel trusting when _____

Uncut Diamond

We all have emotional needs; needs related to having our feelings validated, understood, and believed. Sometimes when these needs are not met, it leaves you feeling sad, worthless, hopeless, and/or unloved. Some say children are like uncut diamonds; their parents and caregivers "polish the diamonds" though their words and actions. Use the list below, and add any you may think of to identify any unmet emotional needs. Discuss with your therapist to come up with an action plan for how these needs can be met – finding ways to polish the diamond.

❏ To feel loved unconditionally
❏ To be recognized for my accomplishments
❏ To be encouraged to do my best
❏ To be listened to, understood, and heard
❏ To feel supported when feeling hurt, weak, or vulnerable
❏ To be treated with respect and dignity
❏ To be forgiven for my mistakes
❏ To feel accepted by those around me
❏ To be trusted and believed
❏ To be treated fairly and equally
❏ To feel capable of succeeding
❏ To feel physically attractive
❏ To feel that I fit in

Inside Out

Let's talk about which feelings we show people and which feelings we keep inside of ourselves. How can you become more aware of the feelings you show vs. those you keep inside? Perhaps, we hide our true feelings and thoughts from the outside world for fear of what others may think.

Think of a time when you hid your feelings inside. Use the t-shirt below to help express your feelings. On the front of the shirt, write or draw how you felt when something upset you, how did you react to the event—what did you show on the outside? On the back of the shirt, write or draw how you felt on the inside.

I Am ...

Have your client go through the list and identify which statements they find to be true, somewhat true, and not true at all. Process together how they decided to categorize each statement. Encourage them to take this chart home and practice saying each statement.

	True	Somewhat True	Not True
I am successful			
I am nice			
I am amazing			
I am honest			
I am happy			
I am confident			
I am social			
I am open			
I am adventurous			
I am generous			
I am peaceful			
I am patient			
I am important			
I am caring			
I am strong			

Your Inner You

This activity is designed to assist you in writing a letter to your "inner you." It is often the inner you, not the "outer you," that carries around hurt, resentment, and guilt. You have done a lot of hard work in therapy thus far: Write a letter to your inner you letting yourself know that it is safe; that it is okay to move past the hurt and sadness.

Dear Inner Me:

_____

_____

_____

_____

_____

_____

_____

_____

_____

_____

_____

_____

_____

_____

_____

_____

Love,
Me

Self-Portrait

Draw a complete picture of yourself. Be sure to include both your positive and negative characteristics. What do you see? Is this what you see or what you think others see? Why do you see yourself in this way? Why do you think others see you this way? What would you change? Why would you make these changes? Who is responsible for making changes? Are these changes that you need or want to make or changes that others think you need to make?

Supportive Responses

Have the child describe their body language and behaviors during times of depressed mood and list these in the space below. Engage in a discussion with the child's therapist to determine if you have noticed these behaviors or body language cues from the child in the past, as well as whether additional ones need to be added. Next, brainstorm helpful and supportive responses that you could offer to the child as an attempt to help improve mood.

Body Language or Behavior	Supportive Responses

Understanding Stress and Support

People have different reactions to stress: Reactions may be physical (headache, sweating), psychological (trouble focusing, sadness), and/or behavioral (nail-biting, yelling). Review the scenarios below, list signs of stress that you experience in each situation, then write strategies that can be used to help reduce stress.

	Physical Signs	Psychological Signs	Behavioral Signs	Support Needed
Starting a new school				
Taking a test				
Losing a game				
Best friend moving away				
Parents having an argument				
Missing the bus				
Field trip being canceled				

	What Can Be Done to Reduce Stress? List Strategies and Individuals Who Can Help You if Needed.
Starting a new school	
Taking a test	
Losing a game	
Best friend moving away	
Parents having an argument	
Missing the bus	
Field trip being canceled	

My Support Constellation

In the stars below, write down the names of five people who are in your support constellation. How have you gotten help from them? How do you reach out to them? Who are you most comfortable with? Do you have a backup person if that person isn't available?

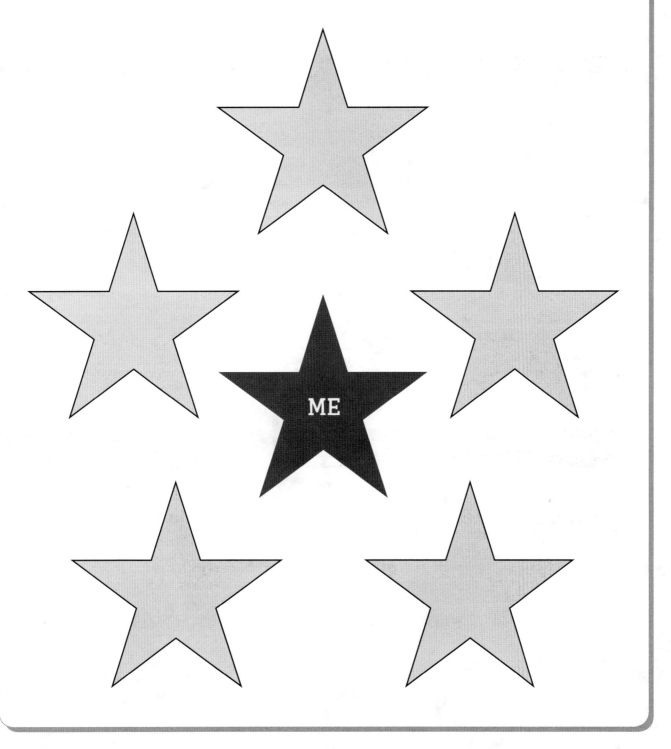

I Like ME!

Use this activity to help recognize your inner strengths. For each block, list a personal quality or strength that you have. Time yourself and see how quickly you can to fill up the entire page.

Awards

The next activity is designed for the caregiver and client to work together to determine positive behaviors to increase and incentives for the client to change current behaviors. For the caregiver, make sure that you have written a positive, healthy, and pro-social behavior in each box that you would like the child to work on. Double check that the award listed appropriately fits the behavior. The awards might entitle older children to a special privilege or younger children to a sticker. Another option is to design/decorate the awards like a badge and make copies to hand out. The child can try to collect as many of these "award badges" as possible. You might consider making these "award badges" worth a certain amount of points to be cashed in for something tangible at the end of the day or week.

Be ready to catch the child engaging in these positive behaviors so that you can hand out these awards immediately. When handing out these awards, use sincere praise and physical affection (e.g., hug, pat on the back, high five). Note how the child reacts to this showering of praise and positive attention. These award moments will serve as a motivator for the child to continue these positive behaviors. Have the child see how many awards they can earn in a day, week, or month. Consider changing the target behaviors and award system with progress and improvement.

Awards

First Behavior

Second Behavior

Third Behavior

I Am Valuable

Reflect on your relationships with others, and complete the following sentences.

My friends
like me because

My parents are
happy when I

I am
happy when

My teachers are
happy when I

I am special because

Reframing Sad Thoughts

In the box below, write down a recent problem you had that made you feel sad. Write about any negative thoughts you had, what you did, and how your body felt. Review what coping skills you could have used. Finally, reframe negative thoughts into positive ones, and write about what you could have done and how your body would have felt after using your coping skills to feel better.

Problem

_____

Negative thoughts I had: _____

_____

Actions I took: _____

_____

How my body felt: _____

_____

Coping Skills

What could I have done differently?
How could I have asked for help?
Who could I have asked for help?

Positive ways I could reframe my thoughts: _____

_____

Actions I could take to cope: _____

_____

How my body would feel after using coping skills:_____

_____

Optimistic Views

This glass is half full rather than half empty. However there are times where it can be difficult to see the positives in a situation. This activity is designed to acknowledge negative thoughts and then "fill the glass" with positive reframed thoughts. Below the glass list a negative thought. Then reframe that thought with two positive thoughts.

Example: Negative thought – *I have no friends.* Positive Thoughts – *I played with Jose at recess today. I may meet new friends at camp next week.*

Negative Thought	**Positive Thought**
_____	_____
_____	_____
_____	_____
_____	_____

Test Your Thinking

Sometimes you may find that it is difficult to stop negative thoughts. They may only stop for a short time and come back. Those thoughts may bombard your brain, but no one else hears them, and no one else challenges them. It can be hard to turn them off or switch to a different thought. It may help you to challenge the negative thought and test your thinking. Fill out the chart below to test your most common negative thought.

1. What is the negative thought you have most often?

2. On a scale of 1 to 10, how strongly do you believe this thought?

3. How and when could you test this thought?

4. If the thought were true, what do you predict would happen?

5. What were the results of the test?

6. On a scale of 1 to 10, how true do you believe this thought is now?

Positive Self-Talk

Anticipatory anxiety can cause individuals to miss out on many positive social-emotional activities. Using positive self-talk is a good coping strategy to enable children to access positive social events and to build confidence. One of the best methods to improve positive self-talk is to use memory. Providing examples of positive self-talk should be followed with "When was the last time you experienced a similar scenario and had a positive outcome?" Use the handout to reinforce the potential for positive outcomes when clients are facing challenging events that could lead to anticipatory anxiety.

On the following worksheet, help the client consider the scenarios listed in the boxes on the left. Invite the client to write a positive self-talk statement in the box to the right of each scenario. Encourage the client to consider personal memories and experiences when developing his/her positive statements.

Positive Self-Talk

Scenario	Positive Self-Talk
Nevaeh was typing a report for work and realized that 2 hours had passed and she was only on the first page. Nevaeh began to feel overwhelmed by the project.	*Example: "In 2 hours, I have finished a page, and I will try to finish one more page before going home for the day."*
Jeremy disliked going out with big groups of people. One of his friends invited him to an art show where there would be a crowd. He wanted to go, but he began feeling nervous about how other people would perceive him. Jeremy began having negative thoughts about the event.	*Example: "I will go and greet my friend and try to talk to one other person while I am there."*
Luis agreed to go on a blind date after a month of his cousin begging him to consider it. He was at the restaurant waiting for his date, and they were 20 minutes late. He was beginning to feel disappointed and rejected.	*Example: "I can still treat myself to a nice dinner if my blind date doesn't show up."*
Laura felt anxious any time she left the house. She needed to go to the store for groceries, and her sister couldn't go with her. Laura began having terrible thoughts about what may happen if she went to the store by herself.	*Example: "When I have left the house before, nothing bad happened."*

The Four Questions

Think of a recent situation in which you had a strong emotional reaction. Use the boxes below to complete the following four questions:

1. What happened?
2. How did you feel?
3. What did you do?
4. What were you thinking? Identify your thoughts, both positive and negative.

What happened?	
How did you feel?	
What did you do?	
What were you thinking?	

Coping Skills Tree

List coping skills that you use when faced with worry or doubt. Imagine them as roots of the tree that help it to be stable and grow strong. Decide whether these coping skills are positive or negative. When have these coping skills been effective? How you can remember to use positive coping skills in the future?

Coping Skill 1: _____

_____

Coping Skill 2: _____

_____

Coping Skill 3: _____

_____

Coping Skill 4: _____

_____

Stoplight Problem Solving

We are presented with problems every day. We have to think about different ways we can handle problems and make decisions about what to do or say. Some problems are easier for us to solve, and others can be more difficult. Obstacles, such as acting before thinking, allowing our feelings to take over, and not seeing any other solutions, may cause us to make poor decisions and not solve our problem. This stoplight activity can help you think about how to solve a difficult problem. Think about a problem you might have, and apply the following steps to it.

Problem Solving Steps

1. **Stop** and think about the problem. Take a few deep breaths.

   What is the situation? _____

   _____

   What are the positives and negatives? _____

   _____

2. **Slow down** and make a plan.

   What could you do/say? _____

   _____

   _____

   _____

3. **Go** ahead with your plan.

   What will probably happen if you use your plan? _____

   _____

Finding Another Solution

Sometimes people become fixed in their thoughts and ideas and struggle to see more than one solution to a problem. We need to become more flexible in our thinking, recognize if the solution we chose is not working, come up with alternative solutions, and consider their potential positive and negative outcomes. In the following chart, think about a problem, come up with possible solutions, and list the positive and negative consequences that might happen. Then, review all of the solutions and consequences you thought of and select the best way to solve the problem.

My problem is: _____

Possible Solutions	Positive Consequences	Negative Consequences
1.		
2.		
3.		
4.		
5.		

The best solution is:

Reaching Out

Sometimes it is difficult to come up with solutions to our problems on our own. We may want to reach out to a trusted adult or friend for support. We can ask them how they would solve the problem or sometimes watch them solving a similar problem. Talk to a trusted advisor about a problem you have or might have, then talk yourself through how you would solve the problem. Use the following chart to write out the steps.

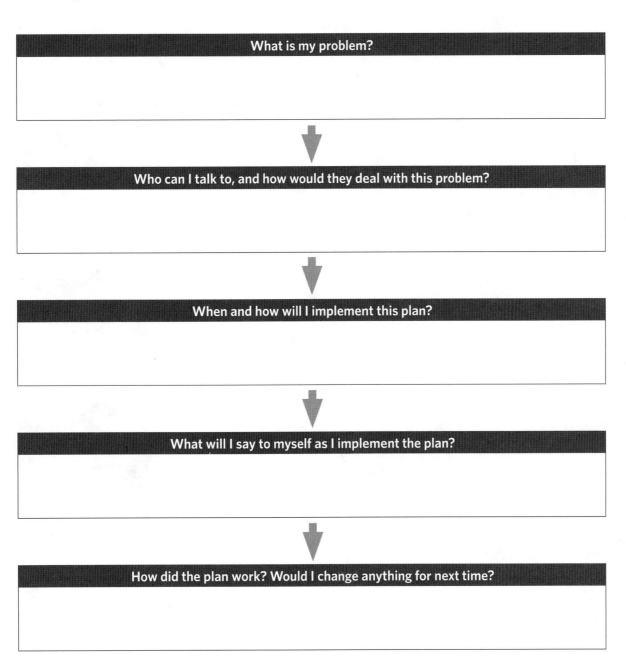

What is my problem?

Who can I talk to, and how would they deal with this problem?

When and how will I implement this plan?

What will I say to myself as I implement the plan?

How did the plan work? Would I change anything for next time?

What Drives You?

It is important to understand what drives you, as this will help you when you are not as motivated. Below, list things that motivate you and things that don't. Also list incentives that keep you working toward your goal and others that don't. Think about ways that you can communicate this to others to help you be more successful. Some examples are listed to get you started.

Motivation

Works	Doesn't Work
Positive peer support	Being timed

What can I do to cope when faced with something that doesn't work? _____

_____

_____

Incentives

Works	Doesn't Work
Teacher praise	Candy

How can I communicate what keeps me motivated to my parents and teachers? _____

_____

_____

Positive Goal Setting

Goal setting is a way to recognize daily accomplishments and keep looking toward the future. Practice setting goals by selecting a small daily goal, a weekly goal, and a future goal (such as a goal for the year). Also indicate what supports you may need to accomplish your goals.

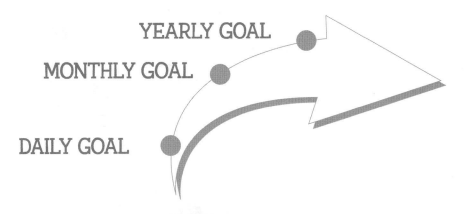

	Declare Your Goal!	Supports Needed
Daily Goal		
Weekly Goal		
Yearly Goal		

Self-Improvement Plan

In order to accomplish your goals and stay accountable, create a self-improvement plan. In the boxes below, identify your current skills, what you would like to be able to do, and set a goal to accomplish. Identify what steps need to be done and give a reasonable date to complete your goal. Place this sheet in an area in which you will see it daily to help you stay on course.

> ### What can I do?

> ### What do I want to be able to do?

> ### My goal is to . . .

> ### I will follow these steps to reach my goal:

I will accomplish my goal by _____

Connecting with Your Body

Connect how your thoughts align with feelings and body responses. Describe a situation in which you felt depressed or worried. Write a negative or sad thought you had in that situation. Use a color to indicate how your body felt in the situation. Positively reframe the thought. What coping skill could be used to help you feel better? Color the second body diagram to show how your body might feel after using a coping skill.

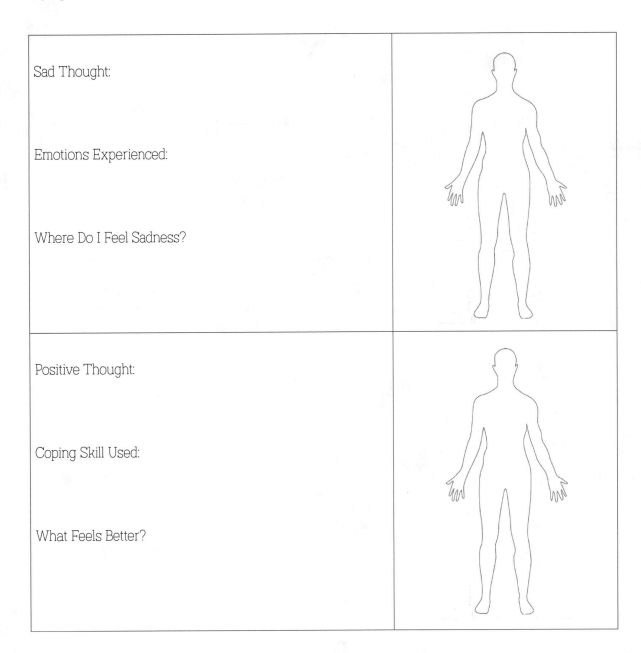

Sad Thought:

Emotions Experienced:

Where Do I Feel Sadness?

Positive Thought:

Coping Skill Used:

What Feels Better?

Making Positive Changes

In the two circles, list changes you can make in your daily life to increase feelings of happiness and to lead a healthier life. List any changes that might apply to both happiness and health in the overlapping portion of the circles.

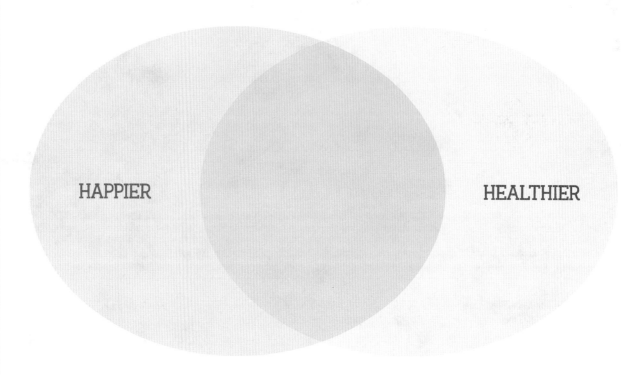

HAPPIER

HEALTHIER

List the Top Three Changes You Would Like to Make

1. _____

_____

2. _____

_____

3. _____

_____

Self-Care Plan

Complete the following questions to make a self-care plan. When you are feeling down, what strategies help you feel better? Create an individual plan to target supports and coping skills to help you increase your mood. Use this as a reminder that you can cope with difficult situations.

1. What do I do now when faced with sad or negative feelings?

2. What are my triggers?

3. What are some positive things I can do when I am feeling sad?

4. Who are some people I can contact for support, and how do I reach them?

5. What things should I avoid when feeling sad?

6. What are three positive sayings I can use to help myself stay calm?

Get Moving!

Physical activity can have a positive impact on mood and help relieve stress. For the next week, make a conscious effort to increase your physical activity. Write down all physical activity you do daily, including what type of activity and how long you did it. Rate your mood before you exercise and after you exercise. Challenge yourself to do some type of activity every day. How does physical activity impact your mood?

Date	Mood Before (1–10, with 1 being awful and 10 being great)	Physical Activity (Name of activity, how long)	Mood After (1–10, with 1 being awful and 10 being great)

Sleep Schedule

Getting a good night's rest can help increase positive feelings during the day. Proper sleep allows you to be more alert, less irritable, and better able to face daily challenges. Write down your current bedtime routine. What helps you relax at night, and what do you need to avoid? Track how much sleep you are getting each night for a week.

My current bedtime routine:

_____

_____

What I need to do to have a restful night sleep:

_____

_____

What I need to avoid to have a restful night sleep:

_____

_____

Day	Wake Up Time	Bed Time	Time Asleep

Emotional Eating

Have you ever used food as a way to cope with your feelings? Write down what foods you associate with each feeling. Also, write an alternative behavior or action you could do to avoid emotional eating. Take note of any emotional eating during the week. Be sure to include how you were feeling, what events set it off, and what you ate. Finally, write a plan to help you avoid emotional eating in the future.

Feeling	Food Eaten	Alternative Behavior
Happy		
Disappointed		
Worried		
Excited		

Day	Feelings	Event	Food Eaten

Plan to avoid emotional eating in the future: _____

_____

_____

_____

About the Authors

Lisa Phifer, DEd, NCSP, is a Nationally Certified School Psychologist who has extensive experience providing school based mental health services to children and adolescents. She earned her doctorate of education in school psychology with and emphasis in neuropsychology at Indiana University of Pennsylvania. Dr. Phifer's work has focused on facilitating student engagement, trauma informed education practices, and advocating for the mental health needs of the students. She is also involved in creating and implementing trauma informed professional development for educators.

Amanda Crowder, MSW, LCSW, is a licensed Social Worker in North Carolina. She has created and adapted evidence-based interventions from cognitive behavioral therapy, mindfulness and solution focused therapy to work with the most challenging children, adolescents and families in difficult situations. She successfully works in multiple settings and consistently delivers interventions that have resulted in client and family engagement and improvement to accomplish therapeutic goals. Amanda believes that everyone has the ability to change and find happiness, and not only find happiness, but deserve to be happy.

Tracy Elsenraat, MA, LPC, ATR-BC, is a Licensed Professional Counselor and a Registered and Board Certified Art Therapist. Since receiving her Master's in Art Therapy Counseling she has been working with a variety of clients from children and women in the corrections system, sexual assault victims to adults with severe mental illness in treatment facilities. She has developed treatment plans and interventions for clients with a variety of mental health needs and helped staff implement treatment. She has served and assisted with the work of various community outreach committees promoting family safety and healthy child development. Elsenraat also provides nationwide presentations on child development, child abuse, neglect, and trauma.

Robert Hull, EDS, Med, NCSP, award winning career educator, special education administrator, professor and school psychologist, is an expert in implementing evidence-based practice into practical, easy to implement strategies that lead to desired outcomes.

Robert's hand-on assistance has helped and inspired thousands of educators who work in the most challenging schools in our nation. His 25 years of experience working with youth and teachers in areas ranging from urban inner cities to impoverished rural counties has led to his recognition by local school systems, state governments, and state legislatures. Robert Hull has a reputation for system/district and state levels, he implemented reforms in the areas of disproportionality, implementing evidence-based practices, and educating traumatized children.

Robert's style uses humor to instill hope and motivation in order to release the anger and disillusionment that those working with challenged youth face. A passionate presenter, he creates optimism while making compelling points. Robert's "get the job done" approach focuses on creating a culture of success where everyone is responsible for leadership and everyone gains from success.